Mary Noel Streatfeild OBE (24 December 1895–11 September 1986), known as Noel Streatfeild, was most famous for her children's books including *Ballet Shoes* (1936). Several of her novels have been adapted for film or television.

Tea by the Nursery Fire

A Children's Nanny
at the Turn of the Century

NOEL STREATFEILD

virago

VIRAGO

First published in Great Britain in 1976 by Michael Joseph Ltd
This paperback edition published in 2012 by Virago Press

A CIP catalogue record for this book
is available from the British Library.

ISBN 978-1-84408-898-0

Typeset in Fournier by M Rules
Printed and bound in Great Britain by
Clays Ltd, St Ives plc

Papers used by Virago are from well-managed forests
and other responsible sources.

MIX
Paper from
responsible sources
FSC® C104740

Virago Press
An imprint of
Little, Brown Book Group
100 Victoria Embankment
London EC4Y 0DY

An Hachette UK Company
www.hachette.co.uk

www.virago.co.uk

Contents

PART ONE

The Child

In the eighteen seventies Emily was born. Her parents, Jem and Betty Huckwell, lived in the tiny village of Easden in the county of Sussex, near enough to the sea to smell it when the wind was right. All round the village were cherry orchards. When Emily was born, so she was told, the cherries were in flower so all the trees were white as if a snowstorm had drifted over them. The old village woman who acted as midwife is said to have remarked: 'The tichy thing, she be likely to 'ave a sweet life born with the cherry blossom in flower.'

Emily's mother might have smiled at her daughter, a quiet woman to woman smile at that, sweet life indeed! She knew that when her little girl was rising thirteen, up would go her hair and off she would be sent to work in one of the big houses, as she had done herself and as her mother had done before her. In time she would marry and start a family of her own, to bring up in the same grinding poverty she had always known. That was the sweet life awaiting Emily.

In those days all the land for miles around Easden belonged

to a family called Pilgrim, though much was rented out to farmers. The Pilgrims lived in the big house and employed many of the local men as farm labourers. Easden at that time was like a toy village bought in a box. There was the church, eleventh century, and the big house which was a mix-up, for the Pilgrims had started to live in Easden a hundred years after the Norman conquest and had been building on to the property ever since. The result was a hotch-potch. The cottages of the villagers lay in a semi-circle round the big house, the church and the village green. If there had been bus-loads of American tourists in those days, the village would have looked to them like a picture labelled 'England' on a calendar. Little white-washed cottages with thatched roofs and in summer roses clinging to the walls. But the cottages were in fact whited sepulchres for most families had at least ten children and there was usually only one bedroom though a few had two. There was no water laid on so water, both for drinking and all other purposes, had to be fetched by the women in pails from the well. They hitched the pails on to a wooden yoke hung from their shoulders. They never complained because fetching water was part of a woman's work, but it was hard going especially when they were pregnant.

The cottages were all tied, that is to say they were part of the men's wages. Many country folk at that date preferred to pay a rent as it was believed, if you accepted a tied cottage, you had to do what you were directed to do, and they preferred freedom to worship as they liked and to vote as they liked, but Squire Pilgrim was different and in most matters left his employees free to do what they thought right, except those of course employed in his house, they had to be Church of England and no nonsense. Outside the ring of cottages there stood the chapel and, if that was their wish, the villagers were free to worship there, not that there was often a service for the village was too small to afford a pastor. But sometimes there would be a wandering preacher. When this happened half the village, whether chapel or not, would turn out to hear him, for, as they would say: 'It was good as a dose of salts to hear what was said about the fires of Hell, proper turned a body out it did.' The Rector was a Pilgrim relation and spent most of his time, according to the season, hunting, fishing or shooting, but come Sunday he was always in church and was usually at a bedside for a death.

The Huckwells did not live in the ring of cottages. As under head gardener Jem was housed in the lodge at the main gate. This had the advantage of giving him and his wife security for their old age. For living in the lodge it was his business to see the big gates were opened to let in or out the carriages or horses of the family and visitors and the tradesmen's carts. Of course Jem did not see to this business himself, he was busy with his gardening, but his wife or, in the holidays, one of the children took on the task. It was a secure home for whoever inhabited the lodge had to be old indeed if they could no longer open or shut the gates.

There were, when Emily was born, three Huckwell children, Albert, Henry and herself. There were to be ten and all lived, a most unusual happening at that date. It was Emily who was to become Gran-Nannie. The family were, she was to say, slightly better off than their neighbours living in the village proper, for Jem earned ten shillings a week whereas everyone else was a farm labourer and for them the wages were eight shillings. At that time ten shillings was usual but two shillings were deducted from the villagers as rent.

All her life Emily remembered her childhood and was able to describe it to her nurslings. The Huckwells were, she told them, a little better brought up than the other children in the hamlet, for her mother, having worked in the nursery of a castle until she married, knew what was what. Most of the village children were 'done up for the winter', which meant sewing them into their clothes in October and leaving them stitched up until the spring, by which time of course the children were crawling with vermin. Betty thought the custom filthy, and though carrying the water was hard all the Huckwells were bathed every Saturday night. Jem thought all that bathing foolish and unhealthy, but he kept what he felt to himself for he never interfered with the way his wife raised his children 'anyway getting roused doant make neither fat nor wool'.

Emily and her brothers and sisters spoke nicely for Betty, having lived in a castle since she was thirteen, had tamed her Sussex accent and she never allowed her children to use it in front of her, though of course they did at school. Jem spoke with the local accent, as he had done all his life, and privately thought the way his wife spoke was caterwomtious or out of the straight.

Emily's mother would laugh remembering life in the castle where she had worked: 'Four of us and in winter a footman to make up the fire and only two to look after.' Then she would smile round at her children not all able to sit at the table but the older ones eating with plates on their knees. 'And the space there was! A great day and a night nursery. It's a wonder what we found to work at but we were always at it, the head nurse saw to that.'

Because Betty had worked in a nursery and had done her best to bring her children up as the castle children were raised Emily, and later her small sister, were the best-dressed little girls in the village. Not for them the plain, long drawers other children wore, theirs were trimmed with lace and feather stitching and so were their petticoats. Her mother still kept in touch with the castle and sometimes a box of cast-off clothes would be sent which served, when altered to fit, not only as pretty frocks and coats but as a guide to the

fashions for the whole village, for though the clothes might
be a year or so out of date they were new styles to the village
and, as once worn by little Lady Helen up at Hunstead
Castle, sure to be the smart thing to wear. Poor villagers,
they did so love dressy clothes but they never had them. In
fact when times were bad with them there were often patches
under their aprons.

With no envy, merely acceptance of the way the world
was run, Betty would tell her children about life in a castle.
'Of course in the nursery we didn't see much of the other
staff except for meals. The head nurse had her meals served
when the children had theirs, but we went down to the
servants' hall for ours, for the head nurse didn't like too
much smell of food in her nursery. Oh my word, it wasn't
half stiff and starchy in the servants' hall. There was nearly
always a great joint, I don't know what was done with it
afterwards, maybe the dogs had it but we never saw it again.
Mr Pettigrew, the butler, always carved the meat with so
solemn a face on him we girls used to say he was like a
parson taking a funeral. It never struck any of them that
great joints of meat should not just disappear when they
were so badly needed in the cottages.'

There was only one meal in the day eaten in the cottages.
This was called tea. Except for the woman of the house and
the babies no one was home midday so the hot meal was
eaten in the evenings. It was almost always bacon dried and

salted when the family pig had been killed, but first there was a roly-poly which was made from flour and boiled in a cloth. The roly-poly was supposed to take the edge off the appetite so no one got a taste of the next course until every fragment of roly-poly was eaten. The main course was built round the small piece of bacon, though sometimes there would be rabbit. Rabbit was not thought highly of in the village where it was called scornfully Egyptian food. Egyptians was the hamlet's name for gypsies. Jem, who saw the Squire and sometimes a guest or two go out for a bit of rough shooting, knew there was often a rabbit in the bag, and he had heard with his own ears the Squire say: 'Tell cook to make a rabbit pie, very good eaten for breakfast is cold rabbit pie.' What was good enough for the Squire was good enough for his gardener, so it was quite usual for Jem to bring home a rabbit in his pocket, and when this happened Betty, though unwillingly, skinned it and served it for the next day's tea.

Whatever little bit of meat there was, and it was very little when shared out, it was cooked with the vegetables. Every cottage had a vegetable garden and often an allotment as well and beautiful vegetables the villagers grew. They were the main support of the families and vast quantities were grown and eaten each in their season. In those days there was no knowledge of out-of-season vegetables, they were all eaten when ripe.

Because Emily's father was second gardener at the big

house and because her mother had worked in the nursery of a castle and so knew what nursery food should be like, the children's meal usually finished with a milk pudding, often rice pudding. The milk came from the Squire's cows and was free for whoever lived in the lodges; it was fetched after school by one of the boys in a big jug. Emily's father would not touch a milk pudding calling it pap, but the children lapped it up. Before and after the meal Emily's father would say grace. 'For what we are about to receive' before the meal and 'For what we have received' after it. Also, after each meal, he would say: 'Doant never forget, you little'ns, whatever work you do when you be grown, see you has your feet under another man's table.'

There were other sources for good food than gardens and allotments. Every woman had a real knowledge of herbs and they helped out: with a bit of home-made lard they could make a wonderfully tasty snack on a slice of home-made bread. Emily's mother started her children's day with a bowl of porridge. 'Get that down you and you'll come to no harm.' The village women, even with milk at a penny a jug, seldom bothered with it. A cup of tea, the cheapest they could buy, and a slice of bread with home-made jam was their idea of how the day should start. All the children old enough for school and all the men took to work with them what was called a 'beever'. This was a bit of pastry filled with whatever the woman of the house could manage –

fruit, vegetables, jam. This was the midday meal. At home the babies would have a mug of milk and a 'piece', which was the slice of home-made bread with herbs or maybe a radish or two, and Betty would have the same.

There was a small school belonging to the village built about twenty years before Emily was born. The Squire, who supported it, charged the parents nothing. He would drop in now and then to see how the children were working. On such occasions the boys stood up and the girls curtseyed and all the children said 'Good-morning, Squir-er'. The children went to school when they were five and the girls continued schooling, as it was called, until they went into service at about twelve years old. The boys who were to be farm labourers stayed on until they were fourteen or fifteen and then went to work, often under their fathers. There was provision for a clever boy or girl to stay on until they were eighteen, but this had never happened. Money was too badly needed in the cottages for such fancy nonsense. The school in fact, run by the Squire with no outside interference, did exactly what he intended it to do. It ensured that every child could read and write, that the girls could sew and the boys do a little simple carpentry, that they knew The Lord's Prayer and The Ten Commandments; above all the Squire expected that children who were taught in his school knew what was called 'their place'. This meant exactly as stated in the hymn 'All Things Bright and Beautiful', 'The rich man in his castle, The poor man at his gate, God made them high or lowly, And ordered their estate'. For years Emily believed the hymn referred especially to her family, for who else in the village lived at the rich man's gate?

Emily enjoyed school though in after years she would admit 'I was never one for book learning'. But she enjoyed owning a slate and laboriously making first rows of pothooks and later the letters of the alphabet on it. Where she shone was at sewing, the teacher told Betty she had never taught a child who sewed so beautifully.

When Emily was seven her only sister, christened Sarah, was born. Oddly enough the village children, who were used to watching animals give birth, were kept away from their homes during the birth of a baby. Neighbours took the children in, and if necessary bedded them down for the night. So Emily did not know at first hand that the arrival of Sarah had caused great anxiety. Of course, through the village children, she picked up the gossip. As for instance that Mrs Folde, she who acted as midwife, was so sure Betty had slipped through her fingers that she wondered where she could find a bit of crepe to fasten on the bees' skep. In those days many families kept a skep of bees, as did the Huckwells. When someone died the head of the house had to tell the bees and fasten a crepe bow to the skep. Another child whispered 'Over twenty-four hours Mrs Folde been at 'er'.

The result of what was evidently a difficult birth was that for the best part of a year Emily was kept out of school to help at home. She missed school but she enjoyed working with her mother. She seemed at that time to have done all the work of the house: baby minding, scrubbing, cleaning, cooking, sewing, for Betty remained what was locally called 'kiddle', which meant frail. The only job Emily did not do was fetch the water, that was too heavy for her so Albert and Henry wore the yoke, and very ashamed they were at being seen doing 'ooman's work!

At the end of the year Betty was again expecting a baby but this time she was not left to the care of Mrs Folde. Mrs Pilgrim came to the rescue. Many times while Emily was running the house she had been down to visit Betty and had had long 'ooman's talk with her. Usually Emily was sent out. 'Wet the tea and then run outside. You can do with a breath of air.' Mrs Pilgrim kept an interested eye on Emily. She was sorry to hear she wanted to be a nursemaid for her children were growing up; what a treasure she was going to be to somebody.

As a result of Mrs Pilgrim's efforts, about two weeks before the baby was born, the wagonette from the big house called at the lodge and Betty, with the travelling basket she had used when in service, was driven away to the nearest town. At that time there were no cottage hospitals so presumably she was given a bed in the workhouse. All Emily knew was that a doctor looked after her mother so well that six weeks later she was home carrying a plump baby boy to be called John. She was no longer 'kiddle' but in a few weeks was as well as before Sarah was born. But – Emily learnt this at school – there could be no more babies.

There were now Albert, Henry, Emily, Tom, Fred, Bert, Patrick, Andrew, Sarah and baby John in the lodge and it was literally bursting at the seams. Also Betty had a hard job to feed the family. So as soon as Albert was eleven he was taken out of school and the Squire put him to work as a trainee gamekeeper. He earned two shillings a week and there were pickings. In the season when there were big parties for the shoots there was a break for lunch and what was considered a snack meal was arranged in one of the big barns on the estate. The food that was eaten made Albert's eyes goggle: pies with every kind of filling, whole chickens and geese, massive cheeses, baskets of bread, pounds of butter and, at the end, what was not eaten was just left. Officially it belonged to the head gamekeeper, but his wife, knowing how many mouths Betty had to fill, would pack a game-bag full as it would hold and hand it to Albert with a whispered 'Your mother can do with a few gobbits'. Albert's two shillings and occasional pickings were a great help but what was really needed was room. So, by the time Emily was ten, Betty began asking around about possible places for her.

'It will be for her own sake as well as helping us,' Betty told Jem. 'That year when I was "kiddle" she got so used to doing things and ordering the others around she never settled down to being a little girl again. I'm not saying she'll go right away but next year maybe when she's rising twelve. Then Sarah can move in along of us and that gives two rooms for the boys.' Emily was just eleven when she went to her first place. She cried bitterly the day before she left when Betty showed her how to put up her hair. It was her great beauty, fair hair almost down to her waist with a curl in it. She never wore it down again.

An advance on the five pounds a year she would earn was allowed. With this money Betty had purchased from the tallyman, who visited the village twice a year, enough print for the two dresses she had to have and a bolt of cotton for her aprons, underwear and caps. She had also bought a length of black serge to make her a Sunday coat. The hat or bonnet the mistress of a house decided her female staff should wear to church was provided. All was packed, beautifully ironed and folded, in Betty's wicker basket called a Pilgrim basket. This had two halves so could be expanded by not fastening the outer basket tight down. It was held in place with a leather strap. Some girls went to their first places with their belongings in parcels; Betty told Emily she could not abide to see that, if she couldn't send her girl neatly fitted out then she wouldn't send her at all.

Emily cried when she left home. She was sad to be leaving but what really hurt was saying goodbye to Sarah. Sarah was just old enough for school and was full of the grandeur of owning a slate. She had no idea why Emily was crying, for no one had gone away in her short life so she didn't know what it meant.

It was the custom for the mothers to see their children off to work and for the neighbours to gather to see them go, and to wave and call out good wishes. Emily was small for eleven and must have looked a funny little thing with her hair up and a cheap straw hat on top of it, as she walked along beside her mother tripping over her first long frock and the new Sunday coat.

There were two ways out of Easden, a two-mile walk to the railway or a short journey to the next village to catch the carrier's cart. This last was the way Emily was to go, for Sir Charles and Lady Pycroft, her employers, lived out in the country in the downlands, well away from where the railway ran.

From what Emily let drop there was no time wasted saying goodbye; if Betty had a job to swallow the lump in her throat she did not show it. She saw Emily seated in the cart, her Pilgrim basket at her feet, gave her a kiss and said: 'Be a good girl now and write regular.' Then she turned away to walk back home.

PART TWO

Nursery Maid

The manor house, called Ernly House, lay in the downs. The carrier dropped Emily at the wrought-iron gates and left her to make her own way up the drive. This was nearly a mile long and with every step she grew more nervous. If only, she thought, she was going to work in the nursery she would have been more contented in herself for she understood nursery work. But on the walk to pick up the carrier's cart Betty had told her that this was not going to happen, at least not at first. There was already a head nurse, an under nurse and a nursery maid in the nursery. What she was engaged to be was maid to wait on the nursery. This, Betty thought, would mean carrying up trays and such like but she was not very sure for, at the castle when she had worked there, an under footman had waited on the nursery.

Emily had said nothing at the time but she had felt a sinking feeling inside; she was on the small side for carrying trays, suppose she dropped one what would happen? Would they send her home in disgrace? The house, when Emily came to it, looked enormous. She could see a front door but there seemed paths round both sides. Luckily there was a young gardener clipping grass round the lawn. In answer to her query he grinned in a friendly way and pointed to the left.

The back door bell was answered by a dark girl who did not look much older than Emily. She smiled and called out 'It's the new girl, Mrs Gosden.'

A warm, fruity voice answered.

'Bring her in then.'

Emily followed the girl through a scullery to a kitchen so large it seemed the size of the church in Easden. At a table Mrs Gosden was sitting, a large-framed woman wearing a huge white apron and a starched white cap. She nodded in a condescending way to Emily.

'You don't rightly belong down here in my kitchen. You were engaged to wait on the nursery but since you are here you better have your dinner. You look as though you could do with a bite, you're no bigger'n a gnat. How you'll manage the trays I don't know. Get her some dinner, Minnie.'

The girl who had let her in darted to an enormous kitchen range, opened the oven doors and took out a huge joint of beef. Emily had been given a beever by Betty for the journey but she had eaten it hours ago, and her mouth watered as she watched meat heaped on a plate together with some brussels sprouts and roast potatoes, the whole covered in thick gravy.

Emily had never seen so much food before meant for one person. She sat down at a side table and ate her way solidly through it.

Presently the kitchen door was opened and in came what to Emily looked a very imposing lady. She did not need the prod Minnie gave her to stand up and curtsey. This, she supposed, was Lady Pycroft.

The imposing one glanced at Emily and said:

'The new girl for the nursery, I presume.'

Emily gave another curtsey.

'Yes, M'Lady.'

The newcomer accepted the title with a slight smile. Shocked, Mrs Gosden broke in:

'This is the housekeeper, Mrs Holthouse,' she said. 'If you should ever have occasion to speak to her you calls her ma'am.' It was clear from the tone she could not imagine an occasion when Emily would speak to Mrs Holthouse.

Mrs Holthouse from then on ignored Minnie and Emily so Emily, who had been raised to respect good food, went thankfully back to her dinner.

Mrs Holthouse then got down to the business which had made her condescend to visit the kitchen. It was all to do with an expected guest who was on a diet, something of which neither woman apparently approved. Minnie took the opportunity to talk to Emily in a whisper.

'You and me are sleeping together. I'll take you up to

show you. You'll have to change before you take up their tea.'

'What are they like in the nursery?' Emily asked.

Minnie shrugged her shoulders.

'I haint never been up there. I knew Polly, the girl what's left, whose place you've taken. She was all right.'

'Why did she leave?'

Minnie's eyes sparkled.

'Sauced Mrs Etheridge, so they say. She's the head nurse and a proper tartar, that Polly said. She's going, stand up and curtsey.'

Mrs Holthouse swept out and Mrs Gosden looked at Emily.

'Finished? Now Minnie can take you up and show you your room. When you're changed come back here and you'll be shown where your things are kept so you can be ready with the nursery tea. Four o'clock sharp Mrs Etheridge likes it on account of getting the children ready for the drawing-room.'

Emily's and Minnie's room was an attic at the top of the house. There were in it two beds, a wardrobe, a chest of drawers, a marble wash stand with a jug and basin, a tooth-brush holder on it and two tooth mugs, beneath was a chamber pot and a pail. All were matching china of the sort bought at a fair. On the wall were two religious pictures. The room felt chilly to Emily used to her over-crowded home.

'I'll have to go,' said Minnie, 'for old mother Gosden has her nap around now, then Edith, the kitchen maid, comes on and we get the kitchen tea. The men see to the drawing-room. Come back to the kitchen directly you've changed or you'll be late with the nursery tea.'

Left alone Emily unpacked and found half the space in the cupboard and chest of drawers had been left for her. She washed and changed into one of her print frocks. Then she put on an apron and pinned one of the little round caps Betty had been told to make to her uneasily piled up hair and she was ready.

Fortunately for Emily all the back premises, which were cut off from the front of the house by green baize doors, had a form of oilcloth for carpeting so she followed this down four floors and came back to the kitchen.

There was a small room off the kitchen which Emily learnt was called the Nursery Pantry. It was from this room she was to collect the dishes to be carried up at meal times.

'There's nothing much tea time,' Minnie said. 'Just a cake and maybe a plate of biscuits. You cut and spread the bread and butter up there. As it's your first time I'll show you the way.'

Minnie carrying a dripping cake and Emily a plate of homemade biscuits and another of delicate sandwiches, the two girls climbed up the flights of stairs, then Minnie led the way through one of the green baize doors and they were in the front of the house with, under their feet, thick carpet. A flight of stairs led to the nurseries at the top of which there was a little gate.

'This has to be kept bolted,' Minnie whispered, 'on account one of the children might fall down.'

Emily, whispering too, asked:

'How many children are there?'

'Four. But you won't have much to do with them. What you got to watch out for is Mrs Etheridge. From what Polly said I wouldn't work for her. Now here's the cake and there's the nursery door, you knock on that. And if Mrs Etheridge speaks to you give her a bob. They like it.'

At first no one heard Emily's gentle tap so she knocked again and this time a small child's voice called out:

'There's somebody knockin' on our door.'

The nursery door was opened by a girl whom Emily guessed was the nursery maid. She was a plump countrified girl with a Sussex burr to her speech.

'Ooh!' she exclaimed to someone out of sight. 'It's our new girl.' To Emily she added: 'I'm Dora.'

An older woman came to the door; there was something of Betty about her which drew Emily to her.

Emily gave a bob.

'I'm Emily Huckwell, ma'am.'

'There's no need to be so formal with me,' the woman said. 'I'm the under nurse, you can call me Ann. Your task is to cut the bread and butter for the children's tea. One plate of white and one of brown.' She looked at Dora. 'Show her the way and as time is running short you can stay and help her.' She turned back to Emily. 'Tea is four sharp as we have to get the children down by five-thirty.'

Off the nursery was a little pantry not unlike the nursery pantry off the kitchen, but in this one Emily noticed there was a sink so probably she washed up there. On the table were two loaves, one brown and one white, a pat of butter and two large plates.

'Twelve slices on each plate,' said Dora, opening a drawer and getting out a couple of knives.

As the two girls cut and spread Dora, in a near whisper, let out a flood of information. At this time of day Mrs Etheridge would be having a nap and it would be someone's business to wake her with a cup of tea. All the high-ups went to sleep of an afternoon. Mrs Gosden and Mrs Holthouse and, of course, Mr Wheatcroft.

'Who's he then?' Emily asked. Dora's voice had awe in it.

'He's the butler.'

'Will I meet him?'

Dora thought about that.

'I expect she'll send you down to morning prayers. You'll see him then though not to speak to, except to say "Good-morning, Mr Wheatcroft, sir," as you pass him at the door. You'll see him in church on Sunday but not to speak to of

course. He lines us up outside the church to make our bobs
to the family.'

When the bread and butter was finished Dora led the way
into the day nursery. It was, Emily thought, a lovely room,
and she felt a lump rising in her throat as she thought how
the little ones at home, Andrew, Sarah and John, would have
loved a ride on the rocking-horse or, indeed, a chance to play
with any of the toys in the room. It was a long room with at
the far end a passage with doors on either side.

'I sleep along there with Ann,' said Dora seeing where
Emily was looking. 'The night nursery is at the end.'

There was a large fire blazing behind a heavy nursery
guard. On the fire a kettle was boiling.

'Do I wet the pot?' Emily asked Dora.

Dora was studying the table.

'No. I'll just tell Ann we're ready. She sits at the top and
I sit at the bottom. Miss Jane sits there and Master Timothy
there and little Miss Ursula sits between you and Ann. Baby
has his bottle and that afterwards.'

Tea was a silent meal. Emily was used to this for at home
everyone was far too hungry to waste time talking. But it
was evidently a nursery rule for when Timothy, who looked
about five, started to say anything Ann gently stopped him.

'We don't talk when we are eating, Master Timothy, do
we? You know what Nannie says.'

The eldest child, Miss Jane who looked about seven, had

a delicate, sensitive little face but when Ann quoted Nannie Emily, who chanced to be looking at her, saw a strange secret look slide across her face. It passed so quickly she might have imagined it but somehow she knew she had not.

After tea all was rush and bustle. Emily only heard what was going on for, having cleared the table, she was given a jug of hot water and sent to the pantry to wash up. She knew when Mrs Etheridge came in for an authoritative voice was added to the others. No doubt Ann told her the new maid had arrived but, if she did, there was no time then to bother with her. So, the washing up finished, Emily stacked everything on her tray and, while waiting for orders, looked out of the window.

There was a lovely view from the back of the house. The gardens stretched away to right and left but directly behind the house was agricultural land. It was early autumn and the corn was ripe. In the far distance stood the Sussex downs, the short turf catching the shadows as the clouds flew by. Emily found her eyes full of tears and it was the cornfield which had put them there. All the women at Easden went gleaning. Even now at home Betty would be planning for it. It happened as soon as the corn was cut and sheaved. Then the children would be kept home from school and all the family, except Jem, would make for the cornfields. There would be plenty of ears of corn the scythes had missed and these all the family picked, trying each sizeable bunch into a small stook. Come dinner time the cornfield became a picnic ground. The babies were fed first, then each family sat down and ate their beevers and drank a mug of cold tea. Later the children would wander away looking for blackberries or maybe a few late wild strawberries for afters. When the fields had been thoroughly gleaned the women of the house would put the family's stooks into a wheelbarrow or, in two cases, an inherited baby carriage and they would be pushed to the miller who, taking his share in payment, would grind it for them. This ground corn used with care was the family flour for the year. There was, I think, no self pity in Emily's tears. She was eleven and, though younger than most girls sent out into the world, she was glad to help her family. That she was going out to work was not discussed with her until it had all been arranged – that was the custom – but oh, alone in that pantry, what a long way off Betty preparing for the gleaning seemed to be.

The children were taken down by Mrs Etheridge who carried six-months-old Master Stephen. Ann followed behind with Miss Ursula and behind her walked Miss Jane firmly gripping Master Timothy by the hand. The door was ajar so Emily saw the procession pass and was amazed. Dora came through from the kitchen and saw her peeping.

'Look all right, don't they? Course that velvet Miss Jane is wearing is only for ordinary. You should see her when

there's visitors. All silk and lace, with her fair hair she looks
like a pharisee.'

Pharisee was the local word in Easden for a fairy and,
hearing it, tears again sprang to Emily's eyes. Dora saw
them and was sympathetic.

'It's awful the first days in service but you soon get used
to it and settle.'

Emily sniffed.

'What do I do with the cake and that?'

'Cake and biscuits over goes in the big tin but you're
supposed to take the bread and butter and sandwiches down,
but you don't. You put them in the fire.'

Emily had never been so shocked.

'I couldn't. Not good food.'

Dora accepted how she felt.

'I couldn't, not when I first came, seems wicked, doesn't
it, when there's so many needing it. But you get used to it.
If you take it down it only gets thrown out. Pity is our pig
can't have it. But take it down if it makes you feel better.'

Scurrying to the kitchen Emily ran into the head nurse
and Ann. Betty had instructed Emily what to do if she ran
into superiors.

'Put your back to the wall and keep your eyes down and
then as they pass give a bob. Most superiors just don't notice
you are there.'

Ann, seeing Emily, introduced her to Mrs Etheridge.

'This is Emily, the new under nursery maid.'

Mrs Etheridge looked as if Ann was pointing out some exceptionally unpleasant insect.

Emily bobbed. Mrs Etheridge looked her up and down.

'You're a very small girl. I need a strong girl to wait on my nurseries but, as you're here, we may as well give you a try.'

Emily managed another bob and to say 'thank you, Mrs Etheridge, ma'am,' but she doubted if she was heard for the nurses had swept on.

Everyone was very busy in the kitchen. A cook called Selina was working at the stove while Mrs Gosden mixed something in a bowl on the table. The kitchen maids, Edith and Minnie, were preparing vegetables, the scullery maids were washing up and continually running in with clean dishes.

'Sorry, dear,' Mrs Gosden said to Emily, 'but you can't come in here when we're preparing dinner. You don't have to take anything up until the nursery supper tray so you best go back upstairs and ask what you can do. If I know Mrs Etheridge she'll find you something. But first go out to the back and throw the bread and that out.'

Emily was dismayed at what she had to do but it was not her place to say anything, so she did as she was told and hurried back to the nurseries. It was cold in the nursery pantry and lonely so Emily went into the day nursery. It was empty but she could hear Ann and Dora talking in the night nursery so she joined them.

The children's baths were given in front of the fire in the night nursery. Hot water, Emily learned, was carried up by the two footmen. The night nursery was another fine big room; it had a frieze of rabbits running round the wall paper. Ann was spreading a piece of towelling on the floor and Dora had just wheeled in the bath tub from where it lived in a cupboard in the passage.

'Is there anything I can do?' Emily asked Ann.

'Yes. Give Dora a hand turning down the beds.'

Naturally at home no beds were turned down so Emily had to learn.

'And we have to be ever so careful,' Dora explained. 'Mrs Etheridge carries on alarming if everything isn't just so.'

'Where is Mrs Etheridge?' Emily asked.

'Gone to fetch the baby. Her Ladyship don't want him long in case he cries or messes himself. Funny gentry are, never seem to want their own children. If I was rich as rich I wouldn't give my baby to a Mrs Etheridge, not ever I wouldn't. When she's got a mood on her she bashes the children.'

Emily, scurrying up and down with her trays of food, had no opportunity to have an opinion of Mrs Etheridge, good or bad, for she scarcely saw her. She did not believe she bashed the children, maybe a smack now and then, but all children got that. Betty, the fondest of mothers, believed in a good smacking when it was deserved. What Emily was beginning to feel was that she was in the wrong job. She wanted what she had always wanted, to train to be a children's nurse, and what chance had she to learn running up and down with trays?

It was expected that all the girls employed in Ernly House would write home to their mothers once a week. The letters home were given to Ann who put them in a wooden box on the hall table with all other out-going mail. From there they were collected, stamped and given to the postman by one of the footmen. Emily's letters were poor, scrappy little things for she was no good at writing. She knew it would be impossible for her to explain why she wanted to change her situation. She was incapable of putting down the words. Then what should she do? She was to have one week's holiday a year, but she would not get that until August or September. There was a chance, so Dora said, that they were given Mothering Sunday. Then, if anything was going in the right direction, they might get home for a night, but it was unlikely in Emily's case that anything would be going Easden way except the carrier's cart, and she had no money to pay for a place in that. Yet to look for another place herself was unthinkable. She must be guided by Betty. But, as she was to learn all her life, there was a force outside herself who planned her future for her.

One of Emily's duties, and the only one which concerned the children, was going with Dora to morning prayers to look after Miss Jane and Master Timothy. The baize-covered door leading to the front stairs was at the bottom of the nursery stairs. They were wide and covered in thick red carpet. Three floors down and they were in the main hall with heads of animals some member of the family had shot scowling down at them from the walls. Master Timothy who, in spite of Dora's efforts to silence him, had chattered all the way from the nursery, had strong feelings against one lion and insisted daily on going up to it and growling at it.

Morning prayers were held in the dining-room. There were chairs arranged round the walls. Four for the nursery party were on the left. A large chair at the top of the room was for Sir Charles with the family Bible open in front of it. At the other end a row of chairs for Lady Pycroft and guests if any were staying. Down the right-hand side were the servants' chairs. Behind them was the great sideboard on which half a dozen or so silver-covered dishes were sitting on warmers. The servants were ushered in by the butler, Mr Wheatcroft. The procession was led by Mrs Holthouse and she was followed by Lady Pycroft's maid and she by the footmen, then came the parlour-maids, house-maids and finished up with the kitchen staff. Mrs Gosden, Emily noticed, did not attend, getting breakfast ready to serve,

Emily guessed. Dora laughed when she heard Emily suggest this.

'Getting dressed more like. She doesn't come down not before 9.30.'

First Sir Charles read a piece out of the Bible. During this Timothy would swing his legs and yawn. Then came the prayers. With a rustle like a wind everybody stood up, turned and knelt at their chairs. The women servants' full-skirted bottoms looking like small hills surmounted with stiff white bows. Timothy was fascinated by this sight and would turn round to look. Sometimes, when his inattention was particularly noticeable, Sir Charles would pause in his prayer reading to glare at him and sometimes he would shout 'Timothy! Attend, sir!! We are speaking to God.' This usually scared even Timothy but on one occasion he had replied: 'I didn't know God was listening,' which convulsed the servants who, in spite of scowls from Sir Charles, so shook with laughter their apron bows quivered. 'I didn't know God was listening' became quite a saying behind the green baize doors.

When Emily arrived it had been holiday time, but Dora told her in school time there was a French lady who came in the mornings to give the children lessons. Emily thought the French lady must be a good teacher for Miss Jane could read anything and even Master Timothy could manage to read and learn the Collect for Sunday.

The children's governess came back at the end of

September. Miss Jane told Emily the news as they walked down to prayers.

'Madame Moulin's coming this morning.'

'Would that be the French lady?' Emily asked.

Miss Jane nodded.

'No more of those horrible morning walks.'

'Don't you go out at all in the mornings then?'

'Yes, but with Madame Moulin. We go as far as the gate and then we are allowed all the way up the drive alone. Don't you love to be alone, Emily?'

Emily was glad to see Miss Jane so happy as she had thought her a rather pitiable child. She was glad, too, that Miss Jane felt she could talk to her.

'Yes, there's times being alone is nice, Miss Jane.'

Emily kept her eyes down at prayers, merely laying a hand on the knee nearest to her when Timothy swung his legs too fiercely, so she did not notice visitors if there were any. But one morning after prayers Lady Pycroft called the children over. She had sitting beside her a young couple who were, Emily gathered, newly married relatives for as the lady kissed Jane she asked:

'How is my bridesmaid?'

It was obvious the lady was going to have a baby.

A few days later when, the lesson over, everybody turned to kneel by their chairs, there was a ripping sound and after prayers, as they all got to their feet to leave, Lady Pycroft was holding a length of her guest's gown which had caught on her chair. Wheatcroft was called over and found an offending nail. Footmen were summoned and the chair carried out and another brought but Wheatcroft, clearly shocked that such a thing should happen at Ernly House, was kneeling by the torn dress.

'Oh dear, madam! I am afraid the dress is torn, there is a nasty jag where the nail caught it.'

Perhaps the lady had not many dresses with her but Emily could see she was upset so, forgetting her position for the moment, she said:

'If I could have your dress, ma'am, I would mend it so that it will never show.'

The house was full of sempstresses, Lady Pycroft's maid heading the list, but the young lady seemed comforted by Emily's offer.

'Oh, would you? I would be so grateful.'

Amused, but prepared to give in to the expectant mother, Lady Pycroft smiled condescendingly at Emily.

'What is your name, girl?' Emily told her. Lady Pycroft evidently relied on her butler. 'See the dress is sent up to the nursery after breakfast.'

Dora, who had been a spectator of all this, climbing the stairs to the nursery, whispered:

'Whatever made you offer? It's not your work.'

Emily, now the little scene was over, wondered at herself.

'I think it was because she looked upset like and her going to have a baby and all, I just spoke without thinking.'

'Silly ha'penth,' said Dora.

As it happened the dress was delivered to the nursery while Emily was polishing the floor. The house-maid who brought it up was new and scared.

'When will it be done? I'm to come back for it.'

Mrs Etheridge was out with Master Stephen and Miss Ursula and so was Ann. There was only Dora to arrange things with. Emily examined the tear. The dress was made from a soft wool material prettily trimmed. It was a nasty tear but no needlework came amiss to Emily, who soon found a place in a seam from which she could pull out a thread for the repair.

'Come back in half an hour. It will be ready.'

Dora, coming into the nursery with an armful of clothes to wash, stopped dead at the sight of Emily sewing at the nursery table.

'Can't you do that somewhere else? She won't half be in a state if she sees what you're doing.'

'It will be done before she's back,' said Emily calmly.

And it was and Mrs Etheridge knew nothing about it. But the result was far-reaching.

Sylvia Burton, to whom the dress belonged, was sister-in-law to Lady Pycroft. She had not thought the marriage a wise one for Sylvia was the daughter of a very well-to-do business family the head of which, her grandfather, had been created a baronet and she had been brought up with luxuries Tom could never afford. He had inherited a property and an income which he could have added to by wise letting of his farms. But Tom was dreamy and artistic, preferring painting pictures to business. Lady Pycroft was prepared to do anything in her power to help the young couple, so when Sylvia said:

'I would like that girl Emily for my nursery,' Lady Pycroft agreed without a thought.

'I'll send for Holthouse, my housekeeper, she will arrange things, but the girl won't be able to take charge of your baby, you know, she's only a child herself.'

Sylvia dismissed that.

'My own Nannie is coming for at least a year. She said she would need a girl to wait on her. I would like Emily. There is something about her.'

Lady Pycroft had thought nothing of Emily with her untidy hair dragged up under her cap. It had been forward of her offering to mend the gown. Still, if Sylvia wanted her she should have her.

'Do not trouble your pretty head, dear,' she said comfortably. 'She is yours. I only hope you are right about her. I can't say she has impressed me.'

Sylvia had made up her mind.

'I know I'm right. There is something about her.'

PART THREE

Under Nurse

A message was received that Sylvia's baby had arrived, a boy who was to be christened John. There was of course a trained nurse in the house for some weeks but they would be glad of Emily, as soon as she could be spared, to wait on the nurse.

There was no question about Emily being spared. The difficulty was how she was to be sent. It was not far as the crow flies to Longton Place, the Burtons' home, but there were winding lanes and it was unthinkable to spare a man and a horse for a whole day merely to transport a nursery maid. In the end a carrier's cart was discovered which, from a not too far away spot, took passengers and parcels to Edenbridge, which was near Longton Place. So one morning Emily with her Pilgrim basket and a box of dainties for the invalid was despatched.

For the size of Longton Place there were not quite enough staff to run it in comfort. There were those mainsprings of any gentleman's residence, a butler and a housekeeper, but the head cook worked with only two girls to help her. There were parlour maids doing the work of footmen, and life would have been easier if there were another housemaid. Nothing disrupted a household more than the outsider who, as the cook said, was neither fish, fowl nor good red herring. Governesses living in belonged to that class but, worst of all, was the trained nurse. Wanting something every five minutes and never thinking to get it for herself. Emily was therefore an answer to prayer. The gardener's boy had gone to fetch her from Edenbridge in the farm cart and the moment she stepped out of it she could feel she was welcome.

'You'll be Emily,' said the head cook. 'I couldn't keep dinner for you seeing it's getting on tea-time, but I've got a nice piece of rabbit pie if you're peckish. The master's fond of rabbit pie,' she added to explain the lowly stature of the food, 'but it's tasty though I says it as shouldn't.'

Emily was longing for a sight of the baby.

'I can manage till tea-time, ma'am,' she said. 'I expect I had better change and then find the nurse. A baby makes so much work.'

So it was less than an hour after she had entered the house that Emily's arms were in the nursery sink scrubbing nappies.

That evening after a good tea, which included the promised slice of rabbit pie, the nurse told her she should tidy up as she was to see the mistress. Sylvia was, as Emily remembered her, lovely as a princess in one of the school story books. The bed had a white canopy and green bows, and there seemed to Emily at first glance to be other green bows on all the furniture. Sylvia, too, seemed a mass of lace and bows. But, and this startled Emily, where was baby? In all the room there was no sign of him, not a bottle nor a toy such as Master Stephen had played with.

'I am glad to see you, Emily,' Sylvia said. 'Nurse is very good but she has baby to see to and has little time for me.'

Emily had to ask: 'Where is baby?'

Sylvia seemed puzzled by the question.

'In the nursery of course. He is brought down when he is being fed. I'm not strong enough yet to be disturbed by his cries.'

Emily thought back to baby John at home. Betty had been up and doing most of the cottage in three days. But she said nothing, she would find a way to get a sight of the baby and maybe give him a good cuddle if nobody was looking.

'I have need of your help, Emily,' Sylvia said. 'At my own home I had of course my own maid. Here things are different; there is not a big staff and the master says I cannot have a maid at present. This means there is no one to brush my hair. Will you come in the evenings and brush it for me?'

Emily had not before met anybody who needed their hair brushed, but she was, as usual, willing to oblige anyone.

'Of course, ma'am.'

From then until the trained nurse left Emily was run off her feet. One nurse and one baby and of course the mistress make three times the work ten of us at home ever made, Emily would think. But if she got tired it was all made worth while by the baby. He was, Emily thought, like a little angel. So quiet, he hardly ever cried, and his little golden head slipped into the crook of her arm as if it were born there. She was in the end allowed to handle John quite a lot, even giving him his bath for, as the nurse said:

'If you want to train as a Nannie you may as well start right away.'

The last week the nurse was in the house they took the baby out in the grounds. Emily had clear starched the robe for this, and over it he wore a pelisse which had a big cape collar. It was not yet May when clothes or clouts might be cast so, though it was a warm day, underneath the robe John wore a vest, a woolly binder, mackintosh knickers over his nappy, wool knickers, a long flannel tied all down the side with sarsonet ribbons and a voluminous starched petticoat.

'And the little lamb never cried once,' Emily reported in her letter home, 'yet he must have felt cruel hot.'

Every evening Emily went down about six o'clock and brushed her mistress's hair. It was during these sessions that she accepted that Mrs Burton, though she knew it was her duty to bear children, was not maternal. However many children she had she was not going to love them as children should be loved. Perhaps, without consciously thinking about it, it was then that Emily gave herself to John. 'You shan't miss any loving if I can help it,' and John seemed to understand.

Sylvia's nannie, Nannie Ludgrove, arrived a week after John's first outing. A large woman, she had been born in London and, when not on her best behaviour, was still full of cockney expressions. She was an unusually clear thinker: 'I speak as I find,' she would say, 'and those that don't like it can lump it. The truth never hurt anybody.'

Nannie, as she wished to be called, liked her nurseries run her own way, but once she had organised this she got on well with the household. She was a tough-looking woman with reddish hair and a dictatorial manner, but inside she had a heart of solid gold. She was not, as she said herself, one for making friends with adults, but with children she was perfect for she ruled by love. She had somehow scaled her thinking down to a child's level, which made her understand immediately what might seem to others an unreasonable request.

Nannie took to Emily. She was so young she could accept her as a child but, as she at once recognised, she had a way with babies.

'You've got a lot to learn, dear, but you've nothing else to do but learn.'

Indeed, with just one baby to look after, it was hard to imagine what two people found to do but Nannie found plenty; they were never idle.

One of the first things Emily had to learn to use was a milk steriliser. This Nannie had borrowed from Mrs Burton's old home.

'There won't be no more babies there and what the eye doesn't miss the heart doesn't grieve after.'

'What's it for then?' Emily asked, gazing with respectful awe at the clumsy thing with holes all round and a thermometer sticking out of it.

Nannie put the steriliser on the fire.

'In the holes we shall put the bottles and that thermometer will tell us when the heat's just right. It means keeping your eye on your fire, you let it go down and down goes your milk temperature.'

Humbly, for fear it was a silly question, Emily asked:

'But Master John doesn't have a bottle, the mistress suckles him.'

Nannie smiled rather grimly.

'I brought Miss Sylvia up from the month. Pretty little thing she was, too, and paid for dressing, but she was never one to put herself out. Feeding the baby is a great tie, she can't go out to dinner or that, so any day now I shall hear she's seeing the doctor and then she'll pitch a tale, anyways the long and short of it will be baby is to be weaned.'

Of course Nannie was right and John was weaned and
Emily took on the job of watching the milk steriliser. She
thought this was the only difference the weaning would
make in her life but she was wrong. When her mistress had
been allowed out of bed the hair-brushing had stopped. But
now that she was starting her social life again she needed, she
said, 'maiding'. There were many big houses within twenty
miles or so where the Burtons went to dine, and the same
families dined in turn at their house, and on party nights
Sylvia wanted her gown removed and hung up, her jewellery
put away and her hair brushed. After dining out, if the house
was some distance away, it would be twelve o'clock before
they were home. The butler, of course, stayed up to see if
his master needed anything, but Emily was a problem. She
slept in a little room next to the night nursery where Nannie
and John slept and calling her might disturb the baby.
Besides, Nannie did not approve. Wearing her sternest face
she went into battle.

'Emily's only a child just turned twelve. You've no right
to have her up at all hours to brush your hair.'

'Then who is to do it?'

'You chose to marry the master,' Nannie retorted, 'and it
was not for lack of warning. You've cut your cloth and you
must wear it. The Baronet, your father, is a wealthy man,
you could have had two maids if you wished. The master is
comfortable, I should say, but it's a tight squeeze for him

running the house and there's no place for fill-falls. You brush your own hair and don't disturb my nursery.'

But Mrs Burton knew her Tom. He could refuse her nothing. A few sulks, a few tears and the day was won. It would be easy for the butler to give Emily a knock as soon as he heard the horse come up the drive.

So Emily, scarcely knowing where she could be so drowned in sleep was she, was waiting more or less dressed in her mistress's room every time she came home from a party.

Nannie, though indignant, accepted what had been arranged. At that date a servant was a servant and had no rights, her only retort was to leave and of course Emily would not do that.

In the servants' hall amongst the younger servants it was mentioned but only in whispers. What was thought about it by the housekeeper and the butler it was impossible to guess. One thing was certain, nothing could be done about it. 'The one who pays the piper calls the tune' was believed in utterly by all servants in the last century.

That summer Emily went home for her week's holiday. The mistress had whined a little when she heard she was going but had perhaps a slightly guilty conscience, for Nannie still disapproved of the hair brushing and did not let her forget it. She showed Emily one of her morning dresses of which she was tired; though soiled, it was, like all Mrs Burton's gowns, fashionable.

'Would your mother like this?' she asked Emily. 'It has a mark or two on it but she can soon get them out.'

Emily was delighted knowing what wearing something fashionable would mean to her mother.

Emily had the reputation in the kitchen for being a good little thing so the head cook, Mrs Pelling, also contributed to her holiday.

'I hear you're leaving early tomorrow,' she said. 'So come down first thing and there'll be a basket waiting for you to take home.'

It was over a year since Emily had been home and, though she had forgotten nothing, she had not remembered how it felt to be so many crushed in so small a space. She had thought so much about the visit home and had supposed the family had done the same. 'Emily comes next week. Won't it be lovely our Emily coming home?'

But it was not like that at all. It was as if water had flowed over the cottage, everything that had been part of her life had been washed away as if she had never been there.

During the week she managed to get back some of her old position. Sitting sewing by the fire she could not tell Betty enough about her work, especially when she had been at Ernly House.

'I was sorry you left there,' Betty told her. '"Never move except to better yourself," your Gran used to say, but from what you've told me you've worsened yourself. I don't hold with gentry who has to cheese-pare and that's how it sounds to me.'

Emily thought of the big nurseries, her own little bedroom, the loaded trays she carried up just for her and Nannie. Then she thought of the main family meal and the joy Mrs Pelling's basket had brought. It was not very exciting by Ernly House standards but there was a big cake, a pound of butter, a chicken and some sugared cakes all luxuries to the Huckwells.

'There was a lot thrown out in Ernly House,' she said. 'I didn't like to see that when so many need it.'

'Gentry always throws out and always will,' Betty stated, 'and there's no arguing with that no more than there is arguing with the east wind.'

Another reason why Betty was sorry Emily had to move to Longton Place was that there were no men servants. She herself had married a gardener, which had meant she could have this lodge. There were always pickings when you were attached to the big house. No doubt even the Burtons would have a coachman and gamekeepers, but where things were on the tight side there weren't so many young men coming up. Not that Betty blamed Emily for leaving Sir Charles and Lady Pycroft; if she was spoken for by a relative then she had to go but it was a pity. Still, she might get another chance. When Nannie left, as seemingly she intended, then Emily could change situations at the same time.

Emily said nothing to this but hugged the memory of baby John to her heart.

While she was at home Emily shared Sarah's mattress in Jem and Betty's room. It was not comfortable for it was too small for two, but this was not what upset Emily. Sarah had grown into an independent child so, if she attempted to cuddle her, she pushed her away.

'Let me be. I'm six so not a baby.'

'It's only a year I've been gone and then you was a rare one for a cuddle.'

'I'm not now, not any more,' Sarah retorted and rolled over.

Nannie Ludgrove seemed to have settled in to her nurseries for there was no more talk of leaving. New babies arrived with fair regularity and each time the trained nurse was in the house Nannie became restless.

'I can't abide her with her fetch this, fetch that,' she would mutter. 'I tell you straight I won't stand her again. I shall go back to her Ladyship. She said when I came here, "There's always work for you here, Nannie, I should be glad of you to take charge of the linen."'

Her Ladyship was Mrs Burton's mother and it was more times than Emily could count that she had heard about the place waiting for Nannie. But somehow Nannie did not leave and Emily began to feel she never would. Though there was much more work as the number of babies increased. John was followed by Henry, then came the first girl, Mary. John was, by the time Mary was born, a sturdy little boy of three. He was a quiet, obedient child and was already trying to read.

'I'll have to talk to Miss Sylvia,' Nannie said to Emily. 'It's time Master John had some learning. She could teach him herself to start with. I can't for I haven't time and you can't because you wouldn't know how, you foggy night you.'

This last was said with affection and Emily knew it.

Usually Emily was told to take Master John down to the drawing-room for half an hour after tea, all changed and washed, but that evening Nannie took him herself.

Sylvia was looking lovely wearing a frilly, lacy tea-gown. She kissed John and gave him a compendium of games to play with.

'I am glad you came down tonight, Nannie, for I wanted to see you. We are going to Ernly House for Christmas. Mary must be weaned by then.'

Nannie thought about Ernly House.

'My Emily came from there, didn't she?'

'That's right. She mended a dress for me and I thought her an obliging little thing so I asked for her.'

'Always was good with her needle,' Nannie agreed. 'Wonder if they've got the nursery staff Emily knew.'

'It's some way off,' Sylvia said, 'but I knew you'd like to know in advance.'

Nannie nodded.

'As I brought you up to know, a stitch in time saves nine. But what I came to tell you was Master John is old enough to start book learning.'

Sylvia turned to look at John busily sorting out the compendium of games. He still wore frocks and looked very small. Tom always teased her that she was too young to have babies, she was only a baby herself and that was how she felt. She didn't want a son who was learning to read.

'I'm sure Mr Burton will say we can't afford extra staff.'

'There's no need for that yet. You could teach him yourself.'

Sylvia gazed at Nannie as if she were a snake who had slid into her Garden of Eden.

'Oh, Nannie, I couldn't! When we go to a dinner, which as you know we often do, I am so tired in the mornings.'

Nannie knew Sylvia often lay half the morning in bed and thoroughly disapproved. That was not the way she had brought her up to behave.

'One day you'll wake up to find you have no cook. I don't know why Mrs Pelling stays, waiting half the morning for her orders.' Sylvia looked sulky, an expression Nannie well remembered from her nursery days. 'Well, it's either do it yourself or ask the Master to engage a teacher.'

'Couldn't you teach him?' Sylvia used her wheedling tone. 'You know you could, you always read beautifully.'

'Fine words butter no parsnips. When do you think I get time for anything? You try looking after a boy of three, another rising two and a baby still in long robes, every inch clear starched and no help but a girl of fourteen. Though I've no complaints of Emily, as good a girl as they come, but she can do no more, even if she was a reader, which she isn't, it's hard enough work for her as it is with her being kept up at night we know what for.'

Sylvia had the shame to blush.

'Oh, very well, send Emily down with him at twelve when you come in from your walk. But not for another two or three weeks. I must have time to send for a reading book.'

'You send, dear,' Nannie agreed, 'but we had a nice book of letters of the alphabet last Christmas. When Emily brings Master John down tomorrow she'll bring the book with her.'

By everyone's reckoning John was a dear little boy. Perhaps rather serious but then, in his baby way, he thought a lot, and when he asked questions, which he often did, he expected them to be carefully answered. Sylvia, though she did try, never understood John. She had not sent to a shop for reading books but asked her mother to send her those she had first learned from. The days had not yet dawned when the upbringing of children was the first consideration in most homes. There was no schoolroom or nursery furniture, children made do with inherited furniture for which no other place could be found. In the Burtons' nursery there was no rocking-horse, dolls' house or elaborate Noah's ark, for such toys were not only expensive but difficult to transport.

In the same way children's books, if there were any, were passed down from generation to generation. At Christmas and for a birthday a book might arrive, but the avalanche of beautifully produced picture books, and for older children, story books, was not yet envisaged. When Sylvia wrote to her mother to ask for the readers she and her brothers and sisters had used, these were sent.

Sylvia's mother was interested mostly in church matters, belonging to that school of low church who thought that saying Gawd rather than God, removed the taint of high church. In her letter to Sylvia she advised that, though John must of course learn his letters first, the best way to educate a child was through The Good Book. He could not be taught too young to study it. It had been, she added, a great sorrow to her that Sylvia had not studied The Good Book as she should. She blamed herself for having engaged the wrong governess, but she had learned too late that her children's heads were being filled with poetry and the plays of William Shakespeare. She hoped that she and Tom read the Bible together daily. She hoped too that, as by next summer the children would be of an age to travel, they would all come to her for a long visit.

Sylvia scowled at her mother's letter. She and Tom went visiting quite often. The thought of taking the children to her home next year was depressing. Too well she knew that nothing of even passing amusement went on in that house. Because she had had a table on which to do lessons Sylvia decided that John must have one. Silver framed photographs and china knick-knacks were, under her instructions, cleared from a table and John was lifted on to a hard chair made high enough by a photograph album and two bound copies of 'Punch'. There he and Sylvia struggled with the alphabet. John was hindered by his eagerness to learn.

'Why is A an apple every day? Could you tell me more things that are A?'

Soon he was demanding to write things, and Sylvia had to drive to the nearest town to buy paper and pencils, and laboriously he was writing out first the alphabet then whole words. He was delighted with this achievement and, since he was not allowed to take his writing book upstairs, always showed his work to Emily when she came to fetch him.

'Look, Emily. I have wrote words an' words an' words.'

Sylvia wanted to be done with lessons, to go up to her room to dress for lunch, but Emily, though sensing this, had not been Nannie's pupil for nothing. Never must there be a feeling of rush or hurry.

'Isn't that beautiful, dear. Give your mother a kiss and say thank you.'

'But, Em'ly, I have a word not finished.'

'You leave it till tomorrow, dear. You'll find it will all be Sir Garnet.'

Going visiting for a nursery party meant turning another nursery into, as nearly as possible, the one left at home. Rooms were given to the guest nurse to be her nurseries. Meals might be taken in the host's nurseries. But this depended on the head nurse and whether or not somebody had been ordered to wait on the guest nursery. It meant a lot of discussion at head of department level but not a whisper of this got beyond the housekeeper. Weeks before packing started in the evenings, when Emily had washed the children's clothes, she and Nannie would sit by the fire repairing any little garment that needed a stitch, while Nannie would cross-question Emily about Ernly House.

'Can you remember clear, Emily? Was it a big establishment?'

Emily remembered vividly.

'Oh yes. There was the head cook, Mrs Gosden, an under cook for the sauces and that, two in the scullery and two to help Mrs Gosden. Of course at the top there was Mrs Holthouse, the housekeeper, and Mr Wheatcroft, the butler. I don't know how many house-maids and parlour-maids but a lot.'

'I shall ask for our meals to be served in our nursery,' said Nannie. 'Little children is better kept quiet with things done their own ways.'

Emily said nothing. In her lowly position she had heard a lot. She knew that here in Longton Place, where there was not as big a staff as might be, there was 'feeling' – to put it no stronger – between Mrs Pelling, the head cook, and Nannie. For even when suitable Nannie refused to agree to the nursery sharing a dish with the dining-room.

'It's true I like chicken for Master John and Master Henry, but I want it same as always, one o'clock prompt. I don't want half cold chicken sent up at half-past one or even later. So she can come off it, we'll have fish the same as I said.'

Much thought was given before the Christmas visit to the children's clothes.

'In a house like that there's new clothes and shoes whenever the head nurse asks. Here Miss Sylvia creates alarming if I ask for half a yard of sarsonet ribbon.'

'What'll you do?' Emily asked Nannie.

'Work on her. I can when I need to. In the end she'll do what I say. What I say is once a Nannie always a Nannie.'

Emily never knew how Nannie talked her mistress into it but she certainly succeeded, for new clothes for all the children suddenly appeared. Nannie was not enthusiastic but satisfied.

'Make a rule, Emily, and stick to it, never show a poor mouth. All the relatives in the family are rich compared to ours. They say fine feathers don't make fine birds, but I'll tell you fine birds can make the less fine feel like sparrows. Put away anything nice for when it's wanted, then the children can visit without shaming you.'

Like all Nannie's precepts Emily stored this away as a squirrel stores nuts.

Though there had been many changes amongst the younger servants at Ernly House the older staff had remained. Sir Charles and Lady Pycroft were not perfect employers but, as Mrs Gosden said, you could go a lot further and fare worse.

After the usual bustle of arrival the nursery party, surrounded by the baggage which included the hip bath packed with toys and clothes, were deposited in their own rooms. There was a large day nursery, a much smaller night nursery and another room for Emily. Nannie, studying the lay-out, decided on changes in her arrangement.

'I don't say it would do for always. But while we're here we'll put the little boys' cots up in your room and I'll just have baby sleeping with me. You'll have to be ever so quiet getting up in the morning for we don't want them running around at six-thirty, but you'll manage.'

Directly the cots were up the children were laid down for an afternoon sleep.

'Won't hurt you lying still even if you don't sleep. You can have a book, Master John, and I'll find you a toy, Master Henry.'

Before tea the housekeeper, Mrs Holthouse, a note-pad in hand came to call. She looked every inch a housekeeper with her black silk apron and bunch of keys clipped round her waist.

'I am Mrs Holthouse. About meals. There's a fine big nursery with room for you all for meals . . . '

Nannie might have been head nurse to a branch of the Royal Family.

'I would not wish to cause trouble but you know how little children are, easily upset by changes, so I would like my children's meals served in here.'

The Burtons were relatives and, moreover, Nannie Ludgrove had been nurse to the Burton children. It was not wise to argue, Mrs Gosden must be pacified in some other way. With a smile which would have looked well on a crocodile she put her pencil to her pad.

'Very well. Now if you would give me some idea what the children like to eat.' Nannie knew what her ideas were on what the children should have to eat. Not that the children always got it at home but now was her chance.

'Breakfast at eight o'clock. We've brought our own steriliser for milk, and I will of course see to the boiling of our own drinking water up here. Baby is still on bottles. I shall not be sieving vegetables for her until next month. The little boys like porridge with thick cream for breakfast followed by bread which has been well soaked in whipped egg and then fried. On this they have little rolls of bacon. Mid-morning they have fruit at this season, it is usually apple well shredded. Lunch at one sharp, they have a jellied or clear soup, fish or chicken to follow then a milk pudding to finish. For tea at four o'clock bread and butter, little sandwiches of jam and a sponge cake. The milk we can get from our steriliser. My under nurse and I prefer a light supper.'

'Morning prayers is at nine if you could spare your girl to bring the little boys down. Usually the children go down to the drawing-room at six. But being Christmas plans will change from day to day and you will be informed.'

'Stuck up ha'porth,' Nannie said to Emily. 'Who does she think she is? "You will be informed." You heard all that, Emily?'

'It's the same nurse I think as when I was here, but I didn't come in to the nursery much. I never cared for her, what I saw of her, nor did the children neither.'

After tea, which was brought up by a footman who said his name was Charles, Emily and Nannie started to dress the children to go downstairs. They were proud of them when, bathed and with clean clothes from top to bottom, they set off for the drawing-room, Emily leading with Master John held by one hand and little Henry by the other, Nannie following carrying Mary wearing one of the new elegant baby gowns. In the front of the house they met other parties descending to the drawing-room, escorted either by the head nurse or, where the children were older, by their nursery maids. Occasionally a small chirping little voice would be raised but it was quietly silenced, so the children descended as if entering church. Emily thought of Master Timothy, no keeping him quiet. Did he still growl at the lion in the hall? Would she see Miss Jane? She must be about ten now and Master Stephen about eight, probably they had left the nursery so were looked after by the governess.

Emily did not have long to wait. No sooner were they inside the drawing-room than Miss Jane, looking a picture in silk and lace, and Master Timothy smart in a frilled shirt and velvet breeches had sprung upon her.

Timothy said: 'We were sure it was you when Charles described what you looked like.'

'Does your hair still fall down?' Jane asked.

'I'm going to boarding-school next autumn,' Timothy told her.

Emily smiled at him.

'Do you still growl at that lion in the hall?' she asked.

Timothy looked at Jane.

'Not out loud he doesn't any more,' Jane said. 'He's too big.'

'But inside I do and it's still Nannie I growl at and I still hate her,' Timothy whispered.

'Do you still do your lessons with the French lady?'

'No,' said Jane. 'We have a German one who lives in the house. But she's gone home for Christmas. We've still got Dora, she looks after Timothy and me. Do you remember her?'

Emily was surprised Dora should still be there, she should surely have gone to a new place and bettered herself by now. Timothy grinned.

'She's got a sweetheart. It's Charles who brought your tea. She's keeping steady company with him. Some day they'll get married and it's going to be in the holidays so Jane and I can go to it.'

The grown-ups were now organising games and soon Emily was watching Master John, in his usual solemn little way, play a 'Ring of Roses.' Then, almost before the games had begun, the children's hour was over and Emily was pulling two sleepy little boys up to bed. It never crossed Emily's or anyone else's mind that there had been a fatiguing amount of dressing-up for so short a visit.

The whole of Christmas seemed to Emily to rush by. On Christmas Day Master John was driven to church with his father and mother and Emily was sent with the servants. She wore the black coat Betty had made her for Sundays and should have worn the little plain black hat Sylvia provided for the household. Nannie and Emily studied this hat anxiously.

'It's not much to start with,' said Nannie, 'and when you plant it on that scullery nob you call hair-dressing it's a sight and no pretending it isn't. You could wear mine but it's no better. Miss Sylvia buys them cheap and they look it, that's the truth of the matter. I'll ask that Charles if there's a carriage or anything going to the shops. If there is we'll get someone to buy some wide black ribbon and I'll trim this up so its own mother wouldn't know it.'

As it happened the dog cart was going in to the nearest shop with all the Pycroft children plus their nurses and Dora.

'Dora looks a soppy ha'porth. Wouldn't know good ribbon if she saw it. You ask Miss Jane to buy it. Better have a yard and a half of the very best quality and one and a half inches wide. We'll give them something to say "Hark the Herald Angels" about. And I'm paying so don't pull a poor mouth at me.'

Emily always remembered that Christmas hat. Nannie had a flair with ribbon and the little black hat became something worth looking at, especially on top of Emily's little face, glowing from the frosty air and shining with the joy of Christmas. There were many glances thrown at her by the men servants and questions asked afterwards amongst the women servants. Mrs Holthouse, when she and the select few were ensconced with port wine and nuts in her sitting-room, dismissed Emily's hat.

'I was not pleased. Young women in service should remember their place.'

Although the nursery party from Longton Place had not seen much of the family or house party it had made a change staying there, and Emily began looking forward to visiting the mistress's family in the summer. Nannie knew the house and family well so it would be like going home to her. Never mind if the old lady was a bit fond of church, Emily liked going to church and a few extra services would do them all good. Another reason why Emily looked forward to the visit was that The Hall was reasonably near her home. It would be possible with a little manoeuvring to catch a carrier's cart. She went home every year for her weekly holiday and enjoyed it. Betty never tired of hearing about Nannie and the children. She still did not approve of Emily working in a house where money was a little scarce, for gentry should be rich, but she could see, if only Emily stayed on until this Nannie Ludgrove left, and if the woman did not hang on too long it could mean Emily might step in as head nurse. She'd manage all right with a good girl under her. Of course she must move on to something better some day, but there was always a place for a reliable head nurse. Of course Emily might marry, but Betty was coming round to the opinion that Emily was not the marrying sort. Emily had an extra reason for hoping to get a day at home. Ever since they had got back to Longton Place Emily had noticed a change in Nannie. She was easily irritated, which was very unlike her, but the cause was equally unusual; she, who was fond of her food, could now only pick at it.

'I don't know what that Mrs Gosden put in the food at Ernly House or maybe she didn't see her saucepans was cleaned proper,' Nannie grumbled, 'but ever since we've been home my food's come back on me.'

Everybody else was in good health so Mrs Gosden did not sound a very likely culprit.

'Do you think you should send for Doctor,' Emily suggested.

The doctor, who drove around in a high gig with his stethoscope inside his top hat, had no surgery. Those who wanted him sent someone to fetch him. He was a fairly regular visitor at Longton Place for there was usually someone requiring his attention. But the fact that you had asked to see the doctor was known by the household in a matter of minutes. So many of the staff preferred to treat themselves rather than become the subject of common gossip.

'You foggy night! I don't need Doctor. What I want is just half an ounce of coriander seeds.'

'What's they?' Emily asked.

'It's a herb that is grown in the garden here when the

summer comes, but not now of course. If I had it I would mix it with a pinch of ginger and another of nutmeg and a little fine sugar and beat them up with my little glass mortar, then I'd throw it back and my wind would break so you would think the windows was blowing out.'

Emily tried to imagine this impressive sound but she was too worried about Nannie for there was no doubt about it, she was kiddle, as they would say in Easden. All she could hope was she would get better soon and in the meantime she would take all the work off her that she could. But it would be a help if she could have a day at home; nobody knew more about herbs and where to find them than Betty. And a good dosing with herbs was likely what Nannie needed.

At first Emily took over the obviously heavy work bathing baby and the two little boys. Sleeping in the nursery with the children and giving Nannie her little room. Taking baby for her morning walk and all three children out in the afternoon. Nannie, looking terrible, would preside at meals but she was careful not to appear until the food was on the table, for someone from the kitchen brought up the nursery meals.

As the weeks passed, that Nannie was getting worse was obvious even to Emily's unskilled eyes. Then one night the climax came. Emily had been up late brushing her mistress's hair and, that finished, had crept back into the nursery and almost immediately fallen asleep. She was woken by John pounding at her.

'Wake up, Emily, wake up. Nannie's makin' a dreadful noise.'

Nannie was – it was screams smothered by blankets. Emily ran to her but could not make her hear anything she said. What was she to do? The person she wanted was the housekeeper or, failing her, the butler, Mr Beck. But where either of these persons slept she had no idea. The only bedroom to which she knew the way was her mistress's. Under Nannie's instruction Emily had bought some warm material and made herself a dressing gown. She pulled this on, gave John a kiss and promised she would only be gone a minute or two, then, conscious it was the wrong thing to do, she ran down the stairs, passed through the green baize door and rapped on Sylvia's door.

It took time to wake the Burtons and then it was Tom, holding a candle, who came to the door. He peered at Emily in amazement.

'What is the trouble? Is the house on fire?'

'It's Nannie, sir. She's in terrible pain, she's screaming, sir.'

Tom went back into the bedroom and pulled the bell beside the fireplace.

'I think it's the nursery maid,' he told Sylvia. 'Seems Nannie Ludgrove is ill.'

'Why tell us?' Sylvia asked. 'She should tell Beck or Mrs Smith.'

Tom came back to the door and repeated what Sylvia had said.

'I don't know where they sleep,' Emily explained. 'I did ought to go, sir, I've left the children alone for Nannie can't do nothing, it's terrible to hear her.'

'Run along then,' Tom said, 'I'll see someone goes for the doctor.'

Emily found conditions unchanged on her return. Nannie was still screaming and John was awake. She raked up the fire and put a saucepan of milk to heat on it, a drop of milk would soon send John off again. The milk had just heated when the outer nursery door was opened and in stalked Mrs Smith. Emily remembered her place. She curtseyed and said: 'Good-morning, ma'am.' Mrs Smith had intended to give Emily a piece of her mind, illness in the household was her concern, it was unheard of to disturb the master and mistress, but she was so shocked by the screams coming from what had been Emily's room that she was silenced. Making worried clucking sounds she hurried across the room and up the passage followed by Emily.

After a quick glance at poor Nannie she drew Emily back into the day nursery.

'Stay here with the children. You can't do anything for her, poor soul. I'll see Doctor's fetched urgent.'

Somehow Emily seems to have arranged to keep the life of the nursery normal. The doctor came and after a shocked look at Nannie asked Emily how long she had been in that condition.

Emily, knowing Nannie did not want her illness discussed, said the condition had only started that night. 'And true, too, as God is my judge,' she had told herself for there had been no screaming when she had gone down to do the mistress's hair.

Somehow an improvised stretcher was made and the doctor, helped by Tom and Beck and supervised by Mrs Smith, got Nannie on to it, covered her in blankets and carried her away.

A message was brought up to Emily by one of the housemaids to say Madam was so tired after her disturbed night she would not be taking the little boys for their reading that morning, so Emily took the three children for a walk. It was late spring and the bluebells were in flower, so she chose a wood not too far for short legs to walk and easy for her to push the baby carriage. Both John and Henry had been told poor Nannie was ill and Henry, who was still proud of new words, at intervals repeated the statement 'Poor Nannie ill', to which, each time he said it, Emily replied:

'That's right, dear. Poor Nannie ill.'

But John, while picking bluebells, turned things over in

his head and presently came to Emily where she sat leaning half asleep against the baby carriage.

'Emily?'

She was wide awake in an instant.

'If Nannie is away ill then will you be Nannie now?'

Emily was startled by the question. Would she? Nannie Ludgrove's training stood by her. Little children had to feel safe, that nothing changed in their nursery.

'I daresay, dear, anyway it'll all be Sir Garnet. You'll see.'

Nannie died. Emily heard talk about an operation but it was too late. She never did know of what Nannie died or where she was buried.

Nannie died in London. Sylvia did not go to the funeral, she told Tom it would upset her, but her mother went and came back to Longton Place with Tom after the funeral. That evening, after Emily had put the children to bed, the outer nursery door opened and, with much rustling of silk, Lady Reeve came in. There was no need for her to introduce herself for she was exactly as Nannie had described her, with her hair severely fastened back under a lace cap, a dress so plain her mother might have worn it if it had not been made of the most beautiful watered silk, partly covered by an exquisite black silk shawl. In the background hovered Mrs Smith, but there was no need for her to remind Emily what was expected of her for she had already made her bob and said 'Good evening, M'Lady'.

Lady Reeve gave a gracious dismissing wave to Mrs Smith.

'You may leave us. I wish to talk to Emily alone. I will find my own way down.'

As the door shut behind Mrs Smith Lady Reeve looked at Emily. She was now rising sixteen and appeared in some ways older. She had at last learnt to manage her hair which she wore in a bun. Lady Reeve pleased Emily by behaving as a grandmother should. She swept across the nursery to the night nursery, Emily following, and by the light of a shaded candle inspected the children. One of Nannie's rules had been that the position in which a child slept was what she had called 'nature's way' and was not therefore to be interfered with. John was lying exactly as she had tucked him in and would be in the same position in the morning. 'Blessed lamb.'

Henry was what Nannie had called rumbustious. Probably, in protest at being tucked into bed, he had flung himself half across his bed with his arms spread wide.

Lady Reeve gently touched one arm.

'Warm as toast,' she whispered to Emily.

Baby Mary was too small to be allowed to sleep as nature intended. She was lying on her side but with her thumb in her mouth.

'I do not like thumb-sucking,' Lady Reeve whispered, stretching out a hand to remove the baby's thumb.

Emily did not of course touch Lady Reeve, it was not her place, but she did say softly 'But sleeping like a little angel'.

Lady Reeve withdrew her hand. The night nursery was spotless, the window a little ajar, which pleased her. She believed in children breathing Gawd's air. She closed her eyes and folded her hands.

'Dear Gawd, bless and guard these Thy children and bring them safely to another day. Amen.'

Emily looked respectful.

Back in the day nursery Lady Reeve sat on Nannie's chair. It had not been used since Nannie had been taken away. Emily thought it was very suitable Lady Reeve should be the first to sit in it.

Lady Reeve had a direct manner of speaking. She acknowledged two superiors – God and Queen Victoria. When speaking to lesser people she spoke either as an equal – though few qualified for this – or as a superior. Naturally Emily was an inferior.

'Nannie Ludgrove, when she was dying, spoke to me about you. She wished you to stay here, eventually to become head nurse.'

There was a pause which Emily felt she was expected to fill.

'I'm powerful fond of the children.'

As if Emily had not spoken Lady Reeve went on.

'You are of course too young for such a position at

present but, with training under a good nurse and constant prayer, you should be suitable by the time you are eighteen.'

Emily thought of Nannie, who had taught her so much, and a lump came into her throat.

'Nobody could never have taught anybody better than Nannie Ludgrove did.'

Lady Reeve accepted that as a compliment.

'A splendid woman. I chose her to bring up my own children and, had Gawd spared her, she was coming back to me to take charge of the linen.'

Emily knew it was not her place to ask questions but she had to know.

'Have you decided who is to come here, M'Lady?'

Lady Reeve shuddered slightly at the impertinence of the question but decided to overlook it.

'You have already worked under her I believe, Mrs Etheridge, head nurse to Sir George and Lady Pycroft.'

Emily managed somehow to control her face. Her Ladyship must not know she had anything against Nannie Etheridge or it was she who would be dismissed and her babies left in the care of that Nannie.

'I was only engaged to wait on the nursery,' she explained. 'Then the mistress came to stay and tore her gown, which I mended, and she asked for me to come as under nurse for the baby that was expected.'

Lady Reeve got up.

'She will be here in two days, a most excellent person. But the children at Ernly House are now in the schoolroom so there will be no real nursery work. The plan for the whole family to come to me in the summer is unchanged so I will see you then.'

One of the housemaids, a girl called Alice of about Emily's age, had been lent to the nursery as a temporary arrangement. She was a good-hearted girl with many younger brothers and sisters at home, so she and Emily had got on happily, Alice doing the rough work, Emily in charge of the children. She came in just after Lady Reeve had left, banging open the door with the tray she was carrying.

'I heard old Stiff and Starchy was up here so I held back your supper till she left. Cold meat again, that Mrs Pelling did ought to be shot, we haven't had a hot supper for I don't know how long.' She noticed that Emily seemed depressed. 'She never gave you notice, did she?'

Emily shook her head.

'No, she was ever so nice. She said I could be head nurse when I'm growed up a bit.'

'Someone new coming then?'

Emily nodded.

'From where I started to work, Ernly House it's called. We went there last Christmas.'

Alice was laying the table. She gave Emily a shrewd stare.

'You didn't like the head nurse?'

'I didn't know her, not really, you see I was employed to wait on the nursery.'

'That's a bum job,' said Alice. 'So you left and came here.'

'Sort of,' Emily agreed. 'You see, the master here is brother to Lady Pycroft and, because I sewed something for her, the mistress wanted me to come here, it was when Master John was expected.'

Alice stuck to her point.

'But you don't like her?'

'It's the children. Here they've been brought up gentle and I thought the little ones at Ernly House wasn't, if you get my meaning.'

Alice was used to a crowded cottage where slaps all round were the order of the day.

'I wouldn't worry. Children is the same no matter where they come from, spare the rod and spoil the child.'

Oddly, this comforted Emily. It sounded exactly as if Nannie Ludgrove was speaking.

Nannie Etheridge arrived two days later. As head of her department she knew her place and expected the rest of the household to know it. As there were no men servants, which she made clear was a discomfort to which she was not accustomed, two of the housemaids carried her luggage and, directly she was settled in, Mrs Smith was up to visit her. John and Henry were playing on the nursery floor, and

Emily had Mary on her knee and was singing one of old
Nannie's rhymes with actions:

> 'A gee-gee and a gentleman
> Went out to ride one day
> Singing horsey porsey, trotty watty
> Galloping so gay.
> But the horse to panic took
> And the man with terror shook
> So they neither looked so happy
> At the ending of the day
> Singing horsey porsey, trotty watty,
> Galloping so gay.'

Mary was cooing and crowing with delight. It was a cosy,
happy scene and Mrs Smith surveyed it with pleasure. But
the new Nannie did not. She distrusted quiet contentment.
What she liked was scenes, repentance, forgiveness. She
would stir things up, she promised herself.

'Take baby into my night nursery,' she ordered Emily.
'Mrs Smith and I cannot hear ourselves speak with that noise
going on.'

It was not Mrs Smith's place to interfere with the heads of
departments but, just for a second, a feeling of anxiety ran
through her. Was this going to be the right Nannie for dear
little Master John and for Master Henry and baby Miss Mary?

Before she returned to her home Lady Reeve had a talk with her son-in-law, the upshot of which was that he would engage a living-in governess.

'You should be able to engage a suitable young woman for very little, especially if she is an impoverished gentlewoman, for suitable employment for them is not, I believe, easy to arrange. If you find the additional wages a strain you must let me know. I will always help, you know that.'

Tom did know and felt loving towards his mother-in-law. He was especially glad that she had so arranged the nursery that Emily was again free to wait on Sylvia. Life was so much more pleasant when Sylvia was happy.

Though nobody knew it or gave the matter a thought Emily was not happy. Nannie was a strict disciplinarian, not because she believed in discipline but she disliked children. She had put up with them when she was under nurse because she could see the place to which she would climb. Once there she need scarcely do a thing. What were under nurses for? Housekeepers, for all they were so high and mighty, had to work hard all the hours there were, if they were not always on the watch something would go wrong. A cook worked like a heathen slave but a head nurse – that was the position to hold. Shut the nursery door and inside her domain she was a Queen with a Queen's comforts. When she had been younger she had considered setting her cap at a butler, but butlers knew too much and, if they married, it was usually a head cook. For what butlers thought about was their stomachs. Emily, under Nannie Ludgrove, had been used to a happy nursery; there would be the prattle of the little boys, only rarely was there a howl. This usually came from Master Henry if he fell or knocked himself. Then Nannie's cosy voice would break in: 'Now then, dear, let Nannie see the damage. There, a kiss will put that right and it'll all be Sir Garnet.' Now the feeling of peace had left the nursery. When Emily was cleaning the grate and polishing the nursery floor before breakfast she would hear sounds from the night nursery, Master Henry calling out to tell the world he was awake.

In time Nannie would answer, not nicely as Emily felt was right, but sharply:

'Be quiet, Master Henry. Nannie will tell you when you can sit up.'

Henry would protest, only to be sternly silenced.

'But, Nannie, I want . . . '

'Then want will have to be your master for if I hear another sound from you, you know what to expect.'

There was a period of uneasy silence broken at last by a loud call from Nannie.

'Emily. Emily. My tea.'

The tea was ready on the tray and, barely giving herself time to straighten her cap, Emily was on her way to the night nursery.

Nannie always looked harassed and cross in the mornings. Sourly she would drink her tea then, putting on her dressing-gown, stump off to dress in a small room down the passage known as Nannie's dressing-room, though it was also the children's washroom and lavatory.

The closing of the door was the signal for lively chatter from the little boys. Emily kissed them and gave John a prayer book open at next Sunday's Collect for the day and Henry a toy.

'Now be good while I see to baby. You know Nannie doesn't like a noise.'

She attended to baby by the nursery fire before going back to the boys, gave both a quick wash, dressed them and had them sitting in their places clean, brushed and smiling as the nursery door was banged open and Alice clattered in with the breakfast tray. The ambition of both Alice and Emily was to get the breakfast on the table before Nannie came to the table. News would be passed breathlessly by Alice.

'There's no cream this morning,' she would whisper, 'but the milk has the top on it. Least said soonest mended this morning. The mistress is having guests to lunch and it seems Mrs Pelling was only told last night.'

When Nannie Etheridge arrived, with any luck Alice was closing the nursery door.

'Always in a rush and tear, that girl,' Nannie would

grumble as she sat down at the head of the table. 'She should give me time to see everything is as I like it.'

There was never a day when everything was as Nannie liked it. The children's food she usually passed as she did not sample it, but her own bacon and eggs, kidneys or kedgeree came in for a lot of criticism and there was never a day when she was satisfied with the way her bread was toasted.

Henry, who was an observant child, would all too often criticise the toast before Nannie did.

'Burnt again,' he would say sourly like a small parrot. 'Mrs Pellin' mus' do it of a purpose.'

'That's all we want to hear from you, thank you, Master Henry,' Nannie would snap. 'No speaking at table, you know Nannie's rule.'

Prayers were at nine and it was Emily's task to take the little boys down. Henry embarrassed Emily by his fondness for the staff. He would always greet the butler, who was holding open the door.

'Go' morning, Mr Beck.'

'Good morning, sir,' Beck would reply.

Then Henry would spot his favourite – Mrs Pelling.

'Good mornin', Mrs Pelling.'

Usually before Mrs Pelling could answer Tom would look up from finding the place in the family Bible.

'Quiet now, Henry, I am starting prayers.'

The moment prayers were over, unless it was raining, the

children were dressed for their walk. There might not be unlimited money in the house but the children still had to change their clothes three times a day. The morning clothes were the plainest, in the afternoon they were a little fussier and after tea it was dressing-up time. Not long after Nannie Etheridge arrived Emily was surprised to hear that she was to take the children for their morning walk.

'I would enjoy the air,' she told Emily, 'but with three children and only one nursery maid I cannot get through my work. I have only one pair of hands.'

Henry, hearing this, had chirruped:

'When Nannie Ludgrove was here Em'ly always took us out for she said she had a bone in her leg.'

'That's enough from you,' Nannie snapped. Then she said to Emily: 'Some little pitchers have too long ears. We must watch out for that.'

Quite soon after Nannie had settled in the governess arrived, a young, nervous little creature called Joan Bun, the daughter of a doctor who had died when she was a baby. Her mother had brought her up in the most rigid genteel poverty, managing to get her accepted as a pupil-teacher in a girls' school for the daughters of gentlemen. Schoolgirls can be cruel and Joan had landed on a bad group. She had always been a shy little thing, but the bullying she suffered in that school had nearly made an idiot out of her.

It was of course Lady Reeve who discovered Joan Bun

and, as much for Joan's sake as for her daughter's, decided she would be a suitable governess for her grandsons. Joan had many qualities in her favour. First on the list, she knew her place, in fact she went further in that direction than a gentlewoman – however poor – should. She was, when Lady Reeve first saw her, kneeling in the church cleaning the brass rods that held the chancel carpet in place. Joan hurriedly and rather untidily scrambled to her feet and gave a little bob.

'Good afternoon, M'Lady.' Joan was nervously twisting her fingers. 'While Mama is finding a place for me she thought I should make myself useful, so I clean the brass twice a week.'

Mrs Bun lived on the Reeves' estates so Lady Reeve knew a Mrs Bun and a nameless daughter existed, but she had thought the girl was still at school. She seemed dimly to remember – perhaps her maid had told her – that the girl had gone to a good school, to prepare her for a position in which she could earn. So thoughtless of the father to have died young for if, as she had heard, he had been a doctor he should surely have seen signs that he was diseased. She looked Joan over. She was deplorably dressed but then she would not wear good clothes for cleaning brass. Although thin she looked healthy and her hair, though screwed up, was a beautiful gold.

'Remind me of your mother's address,' she said. 'Tell her I will call. I may know of a position that will suit you.'

There was a room known as the Library which it was decided should be turned into a schoolroom. And a small bedroom, intended for the personal maid of a visitor, was to be Joan Bun's bedroom. Lady Reeve came to stay for a week to see her protégé settled in. It was always difficult to settle in the first governess. She meant extra work for somebody. In this case that the kitchen had to be responsible for schoolroom trays and Alice for turning out the bedroom, which was a matter for mutterings. 'I should say we had more than enough to do already without waiting on a governess.'

Joan Bun came at exactly the right moment for Longton Place for Sylvia was again expecting. The early days of pregnancy were always difficult for her for she suffered from morning sickness. So whether there was a governess or not she would certainly have refused to give the little boys lessons. So on the morning after her arrival Joan, shaking at the knees, heard the approach of her pupils.

For that first important meeting Lady Reeve was present to make the introductions. Emily was also there, having escorted the little boys from the nursery.

'This is John,' Lady Reeve said, 'and this is Henry.'

Joan looked at her two tiny pupils. She had been told they would be two small boys, but what was small? She had envisaged boys of perhaps seven and ten whom she might not be able to manage, not little fellows of five and three. She could have hugged them but was too scared of Lady Reeve to do more than give the boys a nervous smile.

'I think you will find you have everything you need,' said Lady Reeve, looking at the schoolroom table as if it were the library of a great university. On it had been placed some pencils, an india-rubber, two exercise books, a large Bible, a prayer book and two or three reading books. 'You can write to me' – there was a slight accent on the 'me' – 'if there is anything more you require, but to be able to read Gawd's Holy word is what they mostly need. At the end of two hours Emily will come down for the boys to get them ready for their morning walk on which you will escort them.'

Joan and the little boys spent an industrious but happy morning. John, Joan found, really was advanced for his age, being able to get through, if not to read fluently, the day's portion of the Bible, and Henry surprised her by being past the pot-hook stage and able to write a few words. What Henry could also do, and that Joan tried to prevent him doing, was telling her about the household. At eleven, when Alice brought shredded apples for the boys and a cup of tea for Joan, Henry greeted her with:

'Look, Alice, this is our governess.'

'I know, dear,' Alice said. 'I served Miss Bun her breakfast this morning and her supper last night.'

'Does you eat where?' Henry asked.

It had been hard for Joan to accept that she was to eat

alone. She had hoped for schoolroom meals, except in the evening, but she certainly did not want to discuss the arrangements in front of Alice.

'Eat your apple, dear,' she said.

But Henry had not finished with the subject of Joan's meal.

'Why doesn't you eat with us? Nannie isn't nice but Emily is.'

John seemed to feel Joan needed help.

'Our own Nannie has just died and we don't know the new one very well yet.'

'I does,' said Henry, 'and I doesn't like her.'

Alice and Joan exchanged glances. Joan's look asked: 'Can you go or have you got to stay until the fruit is finished?' Alice's look said: 'I better go or there's no knowing what Master Henry will say next.'

As the door closed on Alice Henry said:

'I likes Alice almost as much as Em'ly but I doesn't like Nannie, if she is cross she . . . '

'Henry,' said Joan, trying to sound severe, 'now, no more talking, finish your apple and then get back to your book.'

Henry did as he was told but with so cheerful a smile it was obvious he did not know he had been reproved.

The boys enjoyed their afternoon walks with Emily but had never enjoyed their morning walk when out with Nannie. They had to hold a handle each of the baby carriage. Emily, used to a home where children wrapped in shawls were put out to play as soon as they could crawl, let the children run free. The estate farms were linked with lanes with little or no traffic on them. Trotting along on the sward, as Emily called the grass verges, the little boys might get dirty but what was the harm in that, Emily would say, it was she who had to brush and clean, and a bit of dirt never hurt any child.

It was on one of these afternoon walks that they met Joan Bun. She was walking aimlessly along, her eyes red as if she had been crying. She came suddenly on Emily with Mary in the baby carriage and the little boys on ahead. The two girls stared at each other awkwardly. Emily felt sorry for Joan for it was a lonesome life she lived, but she had a very strong sense of position and it was not her place to hob-nob with a governess who was halfway to gentry. Joan too knew, for her mother had impressed it on her, that a governess must never forget who she was, under no circumstances to make friends with the servants, but she had been so distraught with loneliness since she came to Longton Place that she just had to talk to somebody, and Emily was not only there but looked kind.

What she had to say spurted out of her like too much water finding its way out of a blocked pipe.

'I thought nothing could ever be so bad as Lindover House, a school for the daughters of gentlemen where I was a pupil-teacher, and that everything afterwards would be better by comparison. But here it is much, much worse. The mornings are all right. I like teaching and they are dear little boys but it's the rest of the day. I try to make the meals last so I have something to do. It's the evenings that are the worst, the schoolroom is so big just to sit alone in and I have nothing to do and . . . '

Tears were pouring down Joan's face. Any minute now the little boys would come running back. Emily tried desperately to think of comfort she might offer.

'Maybe I could think of some way you could come up to the nursery some time of an evening. Can you needle?'

The little boys appeared. Henry flung his arms round Joan's legs.

'You comin' to walk with us?'

'Yes,' said Emily, 'she's come to help me look after you.'

That was the beginning of a less lonely life for Joan. Nannie did not come on the afternoon walks. When the nursery party set out for their walk there was no sign of Joan, but no sooner were they out of sight of the house than she just turned up. Emily, as well as Joan, felt it would be a mistake for anybody to know they walked and talked together. Nowadays it is hard to imagine who they thought would object for they kept their positions. Emily always called Joan 'Miss' whereas Joan called her by her Christian name.

That May there was a heat-wave which turned everyone's minds to their wardrobes. In the nursery no clothes were officially cast because it was still May but Emily, who dressed the children, piece by piece removed flannel binders and woollen garments, hiding them under her own things.

As it happened Nannie Etheridge's mind was on her own clothes. It was not long now before they would be moving to Sir Gerald and Lady Reeve for the summer holiday and for the event she intended to have a new dress, for she had lived in the neighbourhood as a child so she knew many people living round about. As head nurse she considered she had done well for herself and she wanted everyone to know it.

One evening she showed Emily a length of material she had bought for the visit.

'Of course you girls never get out of your uniforms for if you can be spared to go out for a couple of hours, which of course in a nursery cannot happen, you are not allowed beyond the grounds. It is different for senior staff and I must say I do fancy something stylish, makes a wonderful change after all these hollands.'

Emily could see she would be expected to help with the dress and this gave her an idea.

'I don't know nothing about fashion, we never having had the money, our only good things came second-hand from the Castle where my mother worked until she was married. But that governess might know. She's not what you would call smart herself, but she was at a young ladies' boarding school where lots of the girls were ever so rich and dressed beautiful.'

Nannie was so interested in her dress that she did not wonder how and when Emily had talked with the governess.

'Can she draw, I wonder, governesses mostly can?'

Joan was told of the dress the next afternoon and from memory did some sketches of dresses worn by girls at her school.

The drawings were shown to Nannie who was taken with them though worried about a bustle.

'They did say it was going out and now they say it's back.'

'She seems a quiet young lady,' said Emily, 'would you allow her to come up one evening after supper? I'm sure you'd find her helpful.'

That was how Joan was introduced into the nursery. At first it was a temporary arrangement to help with the dressmaking, but soon it was a habit and then the custom. In later years, talking of these days, Nannie said she always tried to get on with governesses, trained nurses and such. It was often their own faults if they led lonely lives, for many thought themselves above hob-nobbing with the nursery.

*

Without Emily there would have been none of the preparations made to go to The Hall that had been made at Christmas for Ernly House. Emily was not at all clear whether, if Nannie Ludgrove had been still alive, there would have been great preparations made. Lady Reeve, for all her money, was not the dressy sort and the mistress, being a daughter, was not likely to dress up to go home but, though nobody knew it, Emily had some treasures hoarded away. Now that the older children were old enough they sometimes went to tea with other children whose parents were friends of their parents. On one of these occasions Nannie had a cold so Emily was entrusted with the children. In conversation with the nurse she had learnt that the family were moving; they were going to live abroad for the health of one of the children. That money was a little scarce at Longton Place was common knowledge so in kindness Emily was approached.

'I wouldn't dare mention it to Mrs Etheridge,' the head nurse said, 'but you won't take offence. We are getting rid of a lot of clothes and that but I've a couple of things just aren't suitable for the village folk.' She had then produced some beautiful little boots 'French hand sewn' she had explained and a silk dressing-gown. 'If you're going visiting they might come in handy.'

'They would.' As it happened Emily never did have charge of a child whom the boots fitted, but how well they looked outside bedroom doors waiting to be carried down to be cleaned. The dressing-gown, used sparingly, lasted for years. It was christened 'Brotherly Love' because all the children shared it. Its first appearance was that summer at The Hall. Nannie showed no surprise at its appearance for Emily had turned up the hem before her eyes and, carefully avoiding an outright lie, had said 'It's kept for going away and that.' The little French boots and the dressing-gown helped her to keep her head high in the way Nannie Ludgrove would have approved.

It had been decided to take Joan to The Hall.

'We have to pay the girl,' Sylvia had told Tom – Joan earned twenty pounds a year – 'so there is no reason to give her a long holiday, if she is not teaching the children she can make herself useful in other ways.' Nannie was delighted that Joan was to join them. If there was someone to lend Emily a hand the more easy it would be for her to go out and visit friends. Because it suited her she was able to be gracious about the sleeping arrangements. The housekeeper, having shown Nannie the nurseries which were unchanged since Nannie Ludgrove had ruled over them, said in a 'I don't suppose you would consider it' voice:

'There is a small spare bedroom at the end of the nursery passage. I could put Miss Bun in there if you would agree. You need not see her, she will eat in her schoolroom.'

Nannie managed to sound wonderfully gracious:

'Of course give her the bedroom and Miss Bun can eat with us seeing it's just for the holiday.'

That holiday was a great success from the nursery point of view. The children lived much more informally than they did at home. There was of course family prayers to which Joan and Emily took the three children. Great efforts were made by Lady Reeve to get Nannie to attend, though she half promised, she never did.

'I find it such a help starting the day with family prayers,' Lady Reeve would say. 'All on our knees to Gawd at the same time. I am sure it makes for a happy home.'

Nannie knew exactly what many of the senior servants felt about family prayers, breaking in as they did on the morning's work, but she kept what she knew to herself.

'If I can manage I will come,' she promised, 'but you know how it is, M'Lady, a nurse's work is never done.'

Actually, since they had arrived at The Hall, she had ordered Emily to bring her breakfast to her in bed.

'You've got Joan to help you. I may as well rest while I have the chance.'

Emily was not by nature critical but more than she knew of Nannie Ludgrove's caustic words had stayed with her. She had heard her mutter once when she did not realise

Emily was listening 'lazy lay-abed' about the mistress and now here was a lazy lay-abed Nannie. What would she have said to that? Back in the nursery she said to Joan: 'I'll sit top of the table this morning, Nannie is having breakfast in bed.' Henry, who was pushing a little cart along the floor, looked up at Emily.

'I would not mind it if Nannie never got up,' he said.

'That is not a nice way to talk, Master Henry,' Emily said gently, then was surprised to realise she agreed with him.

After breakfast Joan took the little boys to the schoolroom where invariably their grandmama would visit them. She would rustle in, a majestic figure in rather out-of-fashion gowns, a lace cap on her head, and enquire how the boys were doing. Joan, in one day, had realised what would please her so would tell John to stand up and read her today's verses from the Bible. Henry was getting on well with his reading but he could not yet manage to read the Bible so instead he repeated parrot-wise a little prayer:

'Matthew, Mark, Luke and John
The bed be blest that I lie on,
Four angels to my bed,
Four angels round my head,
One to watch and one to pray
And two to bear my soul away.'

He added a line at the end.

'And please God could all the angels have guns.'

'What do they want guns for?' Grandmama had asked the first time she heard Henry say this.

'To shoot Nannie,' he replied with relish.

Grandmama did not ask again but she decided she should keep an eye on the nursery.

The Baronet thought nothing of the deplorable habit of putting his grandchildren into a schoolroom all the morning. Time enough for that when they were old enough for school. This was summer time, meant to be enjoyed not only by the children but by that funny little Miss Bun and young Emily. It was his habit to have a glass of port and a Bath Oliver biscuit at eleven o'clock and often he would bring this to the schoolroom, for it was the break when the boys had their fruit, at The Hall home-grown strawberries or a peach.

'Now, Miss Bun,' Grandpapa would wheedle, 'I'm sure it would do the boys good to help me catch a fish.' Or, another day, his suggestion would be a picnic with the food packed in one of the donkey's panniers and Mary popped into the other. Or there was the green cart, a splendid little carriage with a seat either end and excellent steering by spinning round the handles. This, too, was splendid for picnics or it could be used as a toboggan, the children pulling it to the top of the lawn, then climbing on and riding – squealing with excitement – to the bottom.

In the end the Baronet got his way and, unless it was raining, the children were allowed to finish lessons as soon as they had eaten their fruit. Then upstairs they would scamper to be got ready by Emily, then downstairs again picking up Joan on the way to go out and play with Grandpapa. Emily used to watch them from the window and sigh enviously as she got down to clothes washing and ironing.

Mary was the pet of the household. She was a pretty child who, the staff decided, paid for dressing. Her grandmama adored her and sent to London for box-loads of clothes for her. She was, as a rule, a sweet-natured child but she had a stormy temper which would rise up without warning and keep her blazing or sulking until it suddenly died away. That summer her grandmama decided she should tackle this temper and she asked Emily to help her.

'I realise she is now only two but she will soon be three, a very habit-forming age. She must of course be taught to ask Gawd for help. Who hears her prayers?'

Emily was loyal, only she and Joan knew that since they came to The Hall Nannie was not working at all.

'It depends but often I do, M'Lady.'

'Then see that morning and evening she asks Gawd in her own words to help her. Her mamma, when she was a little girl, had something of the same trouble, only in her case it was sulkiness.'

Emily said, trying to sound surprised and to forget words dropped by Nannie Ludgrove:

'Really, M'Lady!'

Since they had arrived at The Hall Emily had scarcely seen her mistress. At The Hall there was plenty of spare staff so a housemaid was ordered by the housekeeper to maid her. Emily was thankful for Sylvia knew a large number of neighbours so she and Tom were constantly out to dinner.

That was a wonderful holiday, there were so many things to amuse small children and doting grandparents to plan for their entertainment, and a large staff only too anxious to help amuse them. Emily, following instructions, saw that Mary prayed about her tempers, at least she said at the end of her prayers 'An' please God help me to be good-tempered', but Emily doubted if she had any idea what she was talking about, for her tempers flared up suddenly and died just as quickly, it was doubtful if she knew she had been bad-tempered. Sundays were the only days which were not looked forward to, for after morning prayers the children had to stay with Grandmama to learn their catechism. John could sail through his as well as prompt Henry. Mary could just lisp 'Honour thy father and mother' but she had no conception why Grandmama wanted her to say it. Afterwards there was the reward of a penny all round, which the children accepted politely in answer to Emily's 'What do you say, dears?' though sometimes Henry would say 'I don't see why I says anything 'cos the penny is not for me it's to put in the plate at church.' After catechism the boys were taken to matins and after lunch to a children's service. Emily had hard work preventing Henry from complaining during the services. In the evenings, when the children were in bed, Emily would settle down to the washing and mending for three children, more or less running wild, made a lot of work. Joan helped her but she was nothing like the needle woman Emily was, so Emily gave her straight forward tasks such as running ribbons through Mary's petticoats and drawers.

Omitting Sundays there was only one flaw in that otherwise idyllic summer. This was the increasingly strange behaviour of Nannie. The older servants no doubt would enjoy a gossip, but Emily was still considered a young girl and there were subjects you never spoke about before young girls. Nannie had, in fact, reached that time of life when if she showed signs of peculiarities, someone was sure to say 'It's her age'. No doubt Nannie suffered quite a lot of discomfort but it had to be borne, no woman in her position would have dreamt of asking help from a doctor for a trouble like that.

Nannie, having spent some years in the village as a child, looked upon the place as if it was home. But the villagers considered her a foreigner. It was true when old

Mrs Grist died, the owner of the village shop, a Mrs Etheridge had taken it on and her husband had worked on one of the farms, but they had only stayed four or five years and had not been greatly liked so they were soon forgotten. Of course they had made Nannie welcome when she first came to call with her being head nurse to Miss Sylvia's little 'uns. But they were busy women and made it clear in their own way that one visit was enough. Nannie, in her nervous and confused state, felt she was lowered in Emily's and Joan's eyes. She could not remember what exactly she had said when they were making her visiting gown, but she was sure she had given the impression that she was coming to the village with a big welcome. So when it had sunk in that there was no welcome, that in fact she was almost forgotten, she took to wandering about the estate rather than go home and admit she had no friends to visit. She must have been very much alone at that time, having no friends among the senior staff in whom she could confide.

As bad luck would have it Nannie's patch of ill-health coincided with someone else's. Tod was a gamekeeper and a good one. A girl had come to stay in the village who was suffering from tuberculosis. Tod, a widower, had fallen for her but she had no use for him and had firmly turned him down. At that time there was no cure for tuberculosis and eventually the girl had died. The village were sorry for

Tod and did what they could to help him, but to no avail. Then suddenly Tod found his own comfort – drink. In a shed where he kept his gamekeeper's equipment he always stowed a bottle or two and, his work finished, he would go to his shed and drink until he fell into a heavy snoring sleep.

One evening when a sudden squall came on Nannie, not knowing whose or what it was, came into the shed to get out of the rain. Tod had just finished work and, glad of company, gave Nannie a drink; this loosened her tongue, it was no time before they realised they needed each other. From that night on Nannie never went to bed sober.

Tod took care of Nannie, he never let her go home so late that the side door, which she used, was locked. He realised she must not have a child and took what precautions he knew.

Joan was a shade more knowledgeable than Emily. Girls at school had talked about brothers who had too much to drink. She would listen to Nannie's stumbling steps climbing the stairs and notice the pulling-herself-together look Nannie put on as she opened the nursery door. There had never been anything said because Nannie made straight for the night nursery and shut the door.

Somehow the girls never by a look admitted Nannie's behaviour was strange. The children were their business and Nannie seemed always to get into bed without disturbing them. Did Emily suspect what Joan suspected? If she did never at any time did she admit it.

Were the grandparents given a hint of what was going on? If so Emily knew nothing about it. One evening the nursery door was flung open and in marched Lady Reeve. The two girls leaped to their feet but she signalled to them to sit.

'You can give me a chair,' she told Emily. Then, sitting down, she asked: 'Where is Nannie?'

Emily hesitated: 'Visiting friends, M'Lady.'

Lady Reeve glanced at the clock.

'So late? I will wait for her.'

It was nearly half an hour later that the girls heard the well-known stumbling steps on the stairs.

'Go to your rooms,' said Lady Reeve, 'I shall see Nannie alone.'

Quickly and quietly the girls slipped away. What happened afterwards they never knew. They hears voices, Mrs Honeysett, the housekeeper, giving orders to one of the housemaids, Mr Johnstone, the butler, clearly appalled at the scandal. Somehow the nursery life was undisturbed for when Emily came in to 'do' her nurseries in the morning all seemed as usual. Only later, when it was time to fetch baby, did Emily discover Nannie's bed had not been slept in. After prayers Lady Reeve sent the boys upstairs with Joan and told Emily to remain.

'This is really your mistress's business but at the present time we do not want her worried. Nurse Etheridge has had to leave in a great hurry, a sudden family illness. We must see how things work out for you are very young, but from today, temporarily, you will take her place as head nurse.'

PART FOUR

Nannie

In the gentle peace of the nursery week faded into week and month into month, all so like each other it was hard to remember time was passing. Except by flowers. Emily had always loved flowers and now she taught the children to love them. The first celandines, a picnic to pick primroses to decorate the church for Easter. Wood anemones, cuckoo flowers and the black-thorn. Then, with a rush, the summer glories, the May trees, the rhododendrons and the azaleas; Longton Place was famous for its azaleas. The hedge banks — still called the sward by Emily — held a royal ransom of flowers amongst which were campions, ragged robins, scabious and poppies. In the autumn there were golden leaves, crimson berries and woolly stretches of traveller's joy. Even winter gave them treasures each year. There were garden expeditions to see the Christmas roses or to search for early snowdrops.

Alice, the housemaid, became under nurse and the two boys had their mid-day meal with Joan in the schoolroom, for Emily was now too busy to supervise a table full. A fat, round, dark-haired little boy called Thomas had succeeded Mary as the baby, and a year later a delicate child christened Matthew had arrived and there was another expected. Still nothing official was said about Emily's position. The household and the children spoke to her and about her always as Nannie, but Sylvia called her Emily when she called her anything at all, but she seemed to avoid her and herself arranged that Alice could take over her hair brushing.

Alice was a gossip and was continually thrusting information on the unwilling Emily.

'Mistress is very poorly with this new little 'un that's expected.'

'She's always kiddle in the first months,' Emily would reply.

'I think she . . .'

'She is the cat's mother,' Emily would reprove.

'Well, I think the mistress wants to get us out of going to The Hall this year.'

'That will be because she feels badly just now.'

'Maybe,' Alice agreed. 'But I think there's more to it. Could be because of you. Her Ladyship always speaks of you as Nannie, as is right and proper, but she never does.'

'She is the cat's mother,' Emily would again reprove.

As things turned out there was no visit to The Hall that year for Tom joined the Army and sailed away to fight the Boers.

Emily often wondered how he had managed to get away for it was the only known occasion when he had gone against Sylvia's wishes. That his becoming a soldier was against her wishes was known to everybody for she wailed her complaints to anybody who was about. Yet somehow Tom won and looking every inch a soldier marched away to be trained, to return on embarkation leave a few months later a captain.

'Doesn't he look handsome!' the household breathed.

Emily shuddered. Suppose it had been John. When he grew up, could there be a war? Then she would whisper words she had learnt from Nannie Ludgrove: 'They hurt your hand when they are little and your heart when they're grown.'

The reason they did not go to The Hall that year was that Sylvia had a difficult birth and only the skill of a new young doctor saved her life and, by a hair, the life of the frail baby who was hurriedly christened Lucy. The house was in a turmoil for the baby had arrived two months early so there was no nurse in the house. Early one morning Mrs Smith in a dressing-gown woke Emily.

'It's the mistress, one of the gardeners has gone for Doctor but she's in labour and is carrying on terrible. Could Alice look after the children?'

'I won't be a minute,' Emily said calmly, 'I'll call Miss Bun on the way. They'll manage without me until the doctor comes.'

The doctor, when he arrived, brought with him the local midwife and together they fought for the two lives, but the doctor who, being new had not met Emily before, at once spotted her competence and kept her in the room. She was, he understood, head nurse so would be a help to fetch anything needed. It was an experience which might have terrified anyone else but Emily took it in her stride. 'It was good I knew what needed doing,' she told Betty later, 'besides you feel more for the baby when you watch the fight it has to get here. When Doctor had delivered little Lucy he just put her down and was back trying to get some brandy down the mistress's throat, so I picked up the little dear, who was still as a little idol, and wrapped her up and cuddled her. The midwife called out "Slap her, girl, slap her", and I did, but before that she was breathing, I knew it, I could feel it.'

Lady Reeve came to look after the disorganised household. At first she was busy comforting her daughter who cried continually for Tom, but as Sylvia recovered she began to see things that were amiss in her daughter's household. With Tom away Sylvia had let the house look after itself. Unless Mrs Smith had been really firm there would have been no spring cleaning, something that was unthinkable. Nothing was renewed; why have the expense of new curtains when there was no Tom to see them? Why bother about food? Why bother about anything? Friends were kind and invited her to stay, but such visits were not much fun for in the country, where life was stricter than in London, there were no dances for grass widows. The only thing that Sylvia enjoyed at that time was clothes. Her wardrobe was stuffed with dresses ready to wear when Tom came home.

One evening when Sylvia was really recovered Lady Reeve tackled a subject her daughter always avoided – the nursery.

'In his letters has Tom mentioned a school for John?'

Tom had but Sylvia was not going to admit it.

'He's only a baby.'

'He is eight and too old to be governed only by women. This autumn he should be sent to Mr Tomkins.'

Mr Tomkins had a preparatory school which Tom had attended as a child.

'It's so expensive,' Sylvia whined. 'I haven't the money.'

'Nonsense!' said her mother. 'You should have less expenses with Tom away. What do you pay Nannie?'

Sylvia looked sulky.

'Emily. Oh, I put her wages up a bit but I haven't made her head nurse.'

'But she is head nurse and a very good one. Persuading Margaret Pycroft to part with her was one of the wisest things you ever did. What do you pay her?'

It took time but in the end Lady Reeve got the full sad

story of her muddled finances out of Sylvia. She listened quietly, working at her embroidery frame, while Sylvia prevaricated, stumbled, corrected herself and finally confessed.

At the end she said: 'Let us start with Nannie!'

Sylvia looked sulkier than ever.

'Fifteen pounds. That's a rise of ten pounds since she came to the house.'

'Let me see, she was just twelve when she came to you, she is now I believe twenty. So she has had a rise which amounts to ten pounds in over nine years and, owing to a shortage of staff, she is doing work no head nurse should be expected to do.'

As a result of that talk Emily was startled to receive a summons to her mistress's bedroom. Alice brought the message.

'She said please ask Nannie to come and see me before she goes out. Nannie, mark you, none of that Emily talk.'

Emily put on a clean apron and cap and, rather shaking at the knees, went to her mistress's bedroom. She paused at the bottom of the nursery flight and looking up at the nursery door whispered:

'Dear God, don't let her send me away. You know I do the best I can and look upon her six like they were my own. Amen.'

Sylvia was all charm that morning but still the invalid.

'Oh, Nannie,' she said in a rather weak voice. 'What must you think of me? I should have raised your salary long ago, but I am raising it now. You will receive fifty pounds a year' – Sylvia's voice grew stronger as she mentioned this – to her and to Emily – enormous sum – 'with back money from the day Nannie Etheridge left, and you will receive a two pound raise every year.'

Emily had not told Betty that Nannie Etheridge had died for, humble as Betty knew herself to be, she would not have accepted that Emily held a head nurse's position without a head nurse's money. Fifty pounds a year was generous, it could have been forty-five. She could now go home – when she felt she could be spared – with her head held high.

Sylvia then told Emily about John going to school. This was bad news but Emily had known it must one day happen. She never had understood the gentry. When the children were small only seeing them one hour a day, what did they know of their loving little ways? When they were older it was governesses. Joan Bun was a nice, good girl but that was only luck, she might just as well have been a French lady teaching the children funny ways like as not. Then, no sooner were the boys eight, than they were packed off to boarding school, nasty rough places so she had heard, where beatings went on. Gentle little John to put up with that.

'I had hoped that maybe he could be kept at home until the master came back.'

'So had I,' Sylvia agreed, 'but it's hard to say when that will be, and I had a letter from the master mentioning the school and now my mother says he should go this autumn. As I have been so ill she is making the arrangements and when we go there in the summer she will take John to a tailor for his clothes.'

Emily could see John in her mind's eye dressed as a little man. She knew if he suffered it would be in silence, not even to her would he complain. Not that she wouldn't know, she and John were so close she knew things about him without words being said. Greatly daring – but, after all, she was a head nurse with a head nurse's right to speak her mind – she said:

'It would be better, ma'am, if you could keep John at home another year, then next year Master Henry would be old enough to go too. It would come easier if they could start together.'

Sylvia got up, she had said all her mother had told her to say.

'You will be seeing her Ladyship, put that idea to her yourself.'

Emily did put her idea to Lady Reeve but she was unable to get her to agree.

'John is a dear, good little boy,' Lady Reeve said, 'and you have raised him beautifully, Nannie, but he has to take his place in the world and for gentlemen the world can be a hard place. His grandpa says his father would wish him to learn to box and he must play games and study Latin and Greek. He has all too little time to study these things for at twelve he will move on to his public school, where his life will be in every way harder.'

'I only hope he stands up for himself,' Emily said.

'With Gawd's help he will learn. He must never forget to read The Good Book every day and to say his prayers. His grandpa, who I am afraid can say very naughty things, said he thought it was more important for John to learn to box.'

When it was time to go for the holiday to The Hall Emily realised she had to face the fact that she had not sufficient help. Joan was coming and so was Alice but with six children, the eldest eight and the youngest three months, Emily just had not got enough hands for she trusted nobody to supervise the packing except herself.

'Why pack these little boots?' Alice asked, holding them up. 'They don't fit none of our children.'

Emily looked fondly at the boots and at Brotherly Love, the dressing-gown. She could almost hear Nannie Ludgrove saying: 'Make a rule, Emily, never to show a poor mouth. They say fine feathers don't make fine birds but I'll tell you fine birds can make less fine feel like sparrows.'

Emily's chief troubles were baby Lucy, who seemed so

frail Emily was thankful each morning when she gave her her first bottle to find she was still breathing, and little Matthew. He was continually ill with attacks of asthma during which he had to be watched, for sometimes his struggle to breathe was too much for him and he lost consciousness.

'I'll wait until we get to The Hall,' Emily promised herself, 'and then I'll have a word with her Ladyship. She must be the right girl or I'd rather manage without.'

Lady Reeve had had strong children and it shocked her that two of Sylvia's children should be so frail. It was understandable perhaps in the case of little Lucy being two months premature, but that Matthew too should be sickly seemed to point to carelessness. There was dangerous talk these days about women having too many children. Such nonsense! What were young women married for except to bear babies? As for Matthew, she was sure there was nothing wrong with him which, with Gawd's help, could not be cured.

The result of all this thinking on the part of Lady Reeve was that she sent for her doctor and had not only Matthew and Lucy but also Sylvia overhauled. The doctor was not young but, by reading, he tried to keep up to date. He still wore a frock coat on his rounds and kept his stethoscope on his head inside his top hat. He was said to be good with children but Emily trembled when he took Lucy in his arms. She knew nothing of hygiene but she did hope he'd not come from an infectious case with baby's little face against his coat.

Surprisingly, he was satisfied with Lucy. He recommended a lot of fresh air and, in a month's time, a little broth and sieved vegetables added to her milk.

'Do not be afraid of rain,' he told Emily. 'When it is wet put her out on the verandah. Before you leave here you should see a great improvement. Whatever you do, the child must not be molly-coddled, she is not made of glass and do not think it.'

The doctor took a much graver view of Matthew. He had read a lot about asthma and had treated several cases.

'He'll have inherited this, Sir Gerald had it, he is out-growing it now but he has a sister who is a martyr to it.'

He told Emily to strip Matthew and he showed her how narrow-chested he was becoming.

'That comes from his struggle to breathe, he hunches forward to give his breath more room. I read something in a medical paper which recommended swimming.'

He saw Emily's appalled expression.

'Do not distress yourself, I have no intention of ordering him to swim in the lake, but I would like him to do some simple exercises. I will talk to her Ladyship about it. There is also something new on the market that you burn which they say eases the breathing. I will order some and will call regularly to see the child. How is his appetite?'

'Some days he does not eat enough to keep a butterfly alive.'

'Then half an hour before his mid-day meal give him a dessert-spoonful of brandy in a little water. Good brandy mind, not the cooking stuff. That will give him an appetite.'

The doctor could not find anything wrong with Sylvia except low spirits.

'What you want, my child, is exercise and a little fun. Do you still ride?'

Sylvia had been quite a good horsewoman but there had been no money for riding since she married Tom.

'Give the girl a horse,' the doctor told Lady Reeve, 'and see she rides every day and, if you can, arrange to pack her off for a month with young people of her own age. That Nannie you have – splendid type – is more than competent to look after the children, so she need have no worries on that account.'

'I do not think she worries,' Lady Reeve said dryly. 'But I will see about the riding and no doubt one of her sisters could have her to stay.'

The Baronet took on Matthew's exercises for he had been taught them when he was small. He was, Emily noticed gratefully, very gentle with Matthew and turned the exercises into play. In fact Emily came to treat him as a confidant. Nothing she could do would make Matthew swallow his brandy; when she succeeded in putting a little down him he promptly brought it back.

'He's only two, sir, so I can't make him see it's to strengthen him.'

The Baronet laughed.

'When I was his age and wheezing like a basket full of kittens I was ordered sherry wine. I couldn't abide the stuff and spat it out. We had a footman to wait on the nursery at that time, good fellow he was, butler now to Duke of Balkham, he helped me out. If no one was looking he drank the stuff in one gulp. "If I'm not here, he told me, give it to that fern of Nannie's." I can tell you that fern liked sherry wine, never saw a plant grow so well.'

What with Matthew and all the other interruptions to nursery life caused by the move, it was nearly two weeks before Emily got an opportunity to talk to Lady Reeve and then, screwed up though she was to bring up the subject, Lady Reeve took the chance from her by talking of something else.

It was after supper, the children were in bed and, it being a lovely evening, Emily had suggested Alice might like a turn in the garden, for she had a suspicion she was sweet on one of the gardeners. For once Joan Bun was not in the nursery but in the room she had been given as a schoolroom, studying a lesson she was to give John and Henry in the morning, for now John and Henry had caught up with her small knowledge and on many days preparation was necessary. Luckily, she thought, it would soon be August when lessons would cease, and come September John would have gone to school and she would only have Henry to trouble with, for Mary was still of the right age for her to cope with.

'Don't get up, Nannie,' said Lady Reeve as Emily half rose from her chair. 'I have come for a little talk. When did you last have a holiday?'

In a flash Emily realised that somehow her Ladyship knew she had not gone home last year, though she would not of course know why.

'It was not easy to get away last year, Master Matthew needing so much attention.'

'And I suppose,' Lady Reeve said, 'you were planning to miss this year because of Miss Lucy.'

Emily nodded: 'And Master Matthew.'

Lady Reeve gave Emily an almost fond smile.

'Everybody needs holidays, Nannie, especially those in your position, the company of small children day in day out can be very wearing. As it happens you can take a holiday with an easy mind. The trained nurse who looked after me when my children were born is coming to live on the estate, and she will be glad to stay in the house and take over your nurseries while you are away.'

Emily thought of the new medicine. She had to burn it on a tin plate when little Master Matthew was choking with asthma and, though Doctor said Miss Lucy was doing well, should she be left?

'I thought I would wait until next year, M'Lady.'

'Nonsense!' said Lady Reeve, 'and if you are anxious at leaving the children put it out of your mind. When my babies were born it was she who brought them into the world for my mama had told me – and quite right too – it was not nice to have a gentleman in the room at such a time, so she never called our doctor.'

Emily met Lady Reeve's old nurse before she left for Easden, and any worries she had at leaving the children rolled off her as if she had been able to lay down a heavy burden. For the nurse, now called Mrs Brackfield, not because she was married but it was the custom to give all senior servants honorary marriage status, was an exact replica of Nannie Ludgrove except that she was much older. When Emily remarked on this she said:

'Well, we were related, she was my mother's youngest sister's child. So when she was fourteen I spoke of her to her Ladyship, for I could see she was nursery type. She started as nursery maid and worked right up; I was not a bit surprised when I heard she was back working, especially in Miss Sylvia's nursery where money was tight, but there, as she said herself, you don't give to get.'

How often Emily had heard Nannie Ludgrove say that. There was a lump in her throat.

Evidently Mrs Brackfield guessed it for she said briskly: 'Now show me all the stuff the doctor's left for Master

Matthew. Then you ought to be getting down for I hear you're to go in the dogcart to where you catch the carrier's cart.'

Emily had a great reception when she got home. Lady Reeve had paid her the money she should have received since Nannie Etheridge's departure. This meant she was able to buy presents for all and to give Betty money. Sylvia, conscious her mother felt she had behaved badly, had given Emily a dress. It was one she did not like, but Emily thought it beautiful. She was not a girl who had dreamed of one day coming home looking like a princess, showering blessings on a family who had never properly appreciated her, all the same there was a difference in her and it was not just the new dress and Betty saw it immediately. Emily, too, knew it for she felt colour glowing in her cheeks and found the saying of Nannie Ludgrove's running through her head: 'Horses sweat, gentlemen perspire, but ladies go all of a glow.' 'Today I must be a lady,' she teased herself, 'for I surely am all of aglow.'

The home-coming was all Emily could have wished. Only Andrew, Sarah, John and Bert were home, for Albert, Henry, Tom, Fred, Bob and Patrick were out at work, as was Jem. On the walk home from the carrier's cart Emily had told Betty her news. She did not mention Nurse Etheridge, she just telescoped time together a little to say: 'That was how I became Head Nannie. I did not get the big rise right away but now I earn fifty pounds a year.'

Betty was so startled she had to stand still to get her breath.

'Fifty pounds! Why, even your feyther doant get that.'

At the gate the children had waited to see their mother and Emily turn the corner; when they did with a whoop they bore down on them, Andrew securing Betty's Pilgrim basket which Emily was carrying.

'Careful now,' said Emily. 'There's presents in there.' Then to Betty she said: 'I thought one day while I'm home we'd go in to the shops, I want my own things now and you'll soon be needing this basket for Sarah.'

Sarah tossed her head.

'I don't want that old-fashioned thing.'

Emily looked at Sarah and marvelled. How she had grown! She was thirteen rising fourteen now and pretty, with lovely fair hair curling at the ends hanging down her back. She was smart too, not in the fashion maybe but not many years out, and was not wearing long skirts as Emily had done at her age but midway between the calf and ankle. 'Quite the young lady,' Emily thought but she said nothing, for an anxious look from Betty warned her not to.

There was no pretending the lodge was not miserably uncomfortable after what Emily was used to. One of the bedrooms had a screen in it behind which was Sarah's bed and this Emily shared. Though more of the boys were working so more money was coming in the family was not better off for space. But somehow, with extra money, they were no better off financially either.

'It's the prices,' Betty explained. 'The farmers can't get nothing for their wheat and every quarter it's the same – someone is giving up. There's I don't know how many cottages vacant and fields lying idle.'

'What happens to farmers then?' Emily asked.

'They goes away most to 'merica but some to Australia. I have the same money to spend every week and a bit more, but it doesn't buy what it did before you was born. And work, why all we had to do when each boy was grown was to tell the Squire or one of the farmers, but now they don't want to know. Why, we sent Bob and Pat to hiring fair.'

'With straws in their mouths?'

Betty nodded.

'But farmers took them, they are both working.'

It was all above Emily's head. In her world, though the Burtons might not have all they could do with, there was always money from somewhere when any extra was wanted. So it was with joy that she pressed five sovereigns into Betty's hand. 'There's a bit to be going on with and I'll be sending more later.'

Never in her life had Betty held five sovereigns. Pay came weekly and was all bespoke before it arrived. Five sovereigns! She could not get over it and maybe it was the five sovereigns that gave her the push needed to speak to Emily about Sarah.

Probably because she was the one girl in a house full of boys, or possibly because she was proud of Sarah and secretly longed to bring her up to be a little lady, Betty had made small effort to get Sarah a place.

'Everything has changed in the eight or nine years you've been gone,' Betty told Emily. 'Carriage folk aren't what they were, at least not hereabouts they are not. Mrs Pilgrim up at the House told me her own self that times were changing, especial in the country. Squire couldn't give away his land so he can't do what he would like for his daughters. You remember Miss Emma, that married an army officer, he that was wounded by one of those Boars, well she's livin' in a small town somewhere, and in her kitchen the cook is single-handed.'

Emily could not imagine a single-handed cook. She only knew the houses in which she had worked or where they had stayed.

'Never! Then who does the vegetables and the sauces and that?'

'The cook, same as I do all the cooking there is here.'

Emily was shocked. Gentry should know their place and never demean themselves and keeping a single-handed cook was demeaning.

Betty gave Emily a few seconds to digest her news, then she said:

'It's time I found a place for Sarah.'

Emily thought about Sarah and knew with every part of her that Sarah would not do for her nursery. Fortunately she had never been one to chatter so, though she had told Betty about the children, especially Master Matthew, she had not mentioned she was looking for a nursery maid.

'What does she want?'

'She won't have nothing except to wait on a lady, see to her clothes and that, but Mrs Pilgrim is suited, she's still got that Mrs Crow she's always had and I can't hear of anyone else.'

Emily gave the matter thought but it was almost time for her to return to The Hall before she came up with a suggestion.

'I will speak to Mrs Honeysett at The Hall. Maybe she would take her when there is a vacancy as a parlourmaid with a view to her maiding visiting ladies. It's true the Baronet has lots of farms but he has a lot else besides so he won't worry himself about wheat.'

Betty must have spoken to Jem about Emily's speaking up for Sarah for the Sunday before she left, when she went outside to smell the morning, Jem was cleaning his boots for work.

'You be a brencheese darter, you be. Though, mine you,

Sarah'll need a middlin' bunt premsley if her doant mend her ways.'

Mrs Honeysett was a good housekeeper though strict. She ruled her household under direction from The Good Book, and spoke, also following her mistress, of God as Gawd. She took her time to form strong opinions about any servant, but she did approve of Emily. So when Emily asked to see her she offered her the hour when the children were in the drawing-room. She gave Emily a chair and listened carefully to what she had to say. Then, after a slight pause, she answered:

'We do not have many parlourmaids here, the men do the parlour work, but we may have a vacancy and when we do ... Is your sister like you?'

Emily thought of pretty, graceful Sarah.

'Oh no. I was never pretty like her nor had her air.'

'Can she sew like you do?'

Emily had to speak the truth.

'I didn't see much of her needling but she was taught by the same school teacher.'

'Do you think she would do well in this house?'

What a question! Emily could be seen clearly fumbling for an answer. At last she said:

'I think she would do anything she had a mind to.'

Mrs Honeysett smiled.

'You are too honest, Nannie. But the first vacancy that

occurs I will give your sister a chance, but nevertheless, if she is not what I want, I shall give her notice.'

All her life Emily believed she had no favourite amongst her nurslings but it was not true. John, since he was born, had been her boy and his luggage, when she had packed it, had soaked up many tears. Such dreadful coarse clothes little schoolboys had to wear. Emily supposed, rightly, she would never again see him in the frilled shirts and velvet breeches he wore to visit the drawing-room. Dark suits the list of school requirements said, and dark suits was what Lady Reeve had ordered the village tailor to make for him. Emily gasped when she first saw them.

'They are so strong they feel as though they would last for ever, M'Lady.'

'Splendid!' Lady Reeve said. 'Boys grow so fast, no doubt these suits will be ready to pass on to Henry when the time comes.'

Emily would like to have packed some personal possessions of John's to give him the feel of home, but he had nothing that meant anything to him except his Bible. Three times he asked Emily if she had packed that, and each time she had replied: 'Of course, dear. As if Nannie would forget it.'

The estate carpenter had made John a tuck box. It had his

name painted on it in bold black letters. The box was sent to the kitchen to be packed but Mrs Pelling told Emily it was a tuck box fit for a little prince.

'Even from London some of the stuff came, chosen by the Baronet himself. I don't know when the young gentlemen eat what's in their tuck boxes. If they're anything like Master John's they could feed an army.'

'It would do our John no good,' Emily said. 'If I know him he'll give it all away.'

'Don't fret,' Mrs Pelling said kindly, 'I know he sometimes seems too good for this world, but I reckon he can stand up for hisself.'

John departed for the station in the dog-cart. To the great envy of his brothers he was to travel by railway train. Something none of them had done. His mother was away visiting so was not there to see him off. It was Nannie with Lucy in her arms, Matthew holding on to her apron and Henry, Mary and Thomas, waving and shouting 'good-bye' that was to be imprinted on his mind and brought out to be looked at when he needed comfort in his first cheerless, lonely days at school.

Emily did not cry when John left but there was a mist of tears dimming her sight. Joan had kept out of sight as John drove away for she knew how Nannie must feel, but she met her in the hall as she was making her way back to the nurseries. Seeing Emily's eyes she whispered:

'He'll do all right, he might even enjoy it.'

Emily shook her head.

'Such a home boy, I can't see that happening.'

Sylvia was trying to arrange they would all go to Ernly House again that Christmas. Emily was against it. The doctor's medicine, helped by a dry autumn, was doing Matthew good. He had now started lessons and would come back proudly to the nursery to show Emily a row of pothooks. He could also, with help, manage to read a few words from his school-book called 'Reading Without Tears'. Then there was Thomas. He was proving the clever one of the family, but Joan did not altogether approve of his cleverness.

'It's not natural,' she told Emily. 'When I'm teaching Henry and Mary he takes in every word and comes out with it later. And him not four years old.'

'There are children like that,' Emily said calmly. 'My brother Fred was that way but he out-grew it and so will Thomas, you'll see.'

Thomas was sharp in other ways than lessons, he picked up what people said. After talking to one of the gardeners he came out with:

'An' there I were all of a muck swet.'

Emily was shocked but she did not show it, merely repeating the saying much used by Nannie Ludgrove:

'Horses sweat, gentlemen perspire and ladies go all of a glow.'

Alice had suffocated a giggle when Thomas had quoted the gardener, but when Emily capped it she thought to herself:

'Too sharp by half, young Master Thomas is, if he isn't careful he'll cut himself.'

Then there was Mary to consider, still battling unsuccessfully with her temper. She could be as good as gold one minute and the next beating Thomas's or Henry's heads on the floor shouting: 'You pig, you beast!'

The tempers disappeared almost as soon as they had flared up, often before Emily had time to know what the trouble had been. But it would be a disgrace if she behaved that way at Ernly House.

Although Lady Reeve had agreed to pay the wages of a new girl she was finding it very difficult to hear of one. She wrote to Emily about it. 'I keep hearing of girls who need places but none appears to wish to work in a nursery. I do not know what the world is coming to.'

The day before the family left for Christmas John came home from school. He had come by train and been met at the station and driven home. Though he did not know it Sylvia, trying to do the right thing, had tea waiting for him in the drawing-room. But the carriage had no sooner stopped at the door than John was out of it, and hareing up the stairs to the nursery to fling his arms round Emily.

For a minute Emily forgot everything except the joy of having him back. Then she remembered the mistress waiting in the drawing-room. She gave John a little push.

'You're to have tea with your mama in the drawing-room.'

John seemed not to hear her. He ran round the tea-table rubbing Henry's hair the wrong way, kissing Mary, patting Thomas and gently hugging Matthew.

'Where's Lucy?' he asked.

'Sleeping in her cot,' said Emily, 'and I don't want her woken yet. Now run along down to your mama. She won't like to be kept waiting.'

John, as usual, did what he was told but it was an awkward little tea party. Sylvia was never to understand that if you give your children to another to bring up you cannot casually take them back. She asked all the usual questions.

'Was he happy at school? Had he made any friends? Was the food good? Had he written to his papa?'

John enjoyed his food after the usual sparse school diet and was able to answer all the questions to Sylvia's satisfaction, but when she said she must go and supervise her packing, as they were leaving early in the morning, he sprang eagerly to his feet, apparently to hold the door open for her, but really to get back to the nursery.

Because of the departure the next day there was no going downstairs that evening. Instead Joan had the children gathered round the table playing Happy Families, while Emily gave Lucy her bottle and Alice turned down the beds.

Now the first joy of seeing him again was over Emily was able to study John. He was, she thought, thinner but that was probably all those rough games young gentlemen played and that boxing his papa was so set on. But in John himself there seemed no change, he was the same loving little boy with an extra glow from his gladness at being home.

It was while they were at Ernly House that Emily noticed that Joan was changing. There had been heavy snow falls and hard frosts and all the children old enough, and all the adults young enough, were out tobogganing or skating all the daylight hours. John and Henry were never seen until tea-time and even Mary and Thomas were allowed, accompanied by Alice, to play in the snow in place of formal walks. This meant that Emily and Joan spent most of the day together looking after Matthew and Lucy. It was this that made Emily notice that Joan was lapsy, a Sussex expression which would have shocked Betty if she had heard Emily using it, even in her head. Thinking it over Emily supposed that Joan might have been lapsy, that was to say on the lazy, slow side, for some while and she, with so much to do, had not noticed. Now that she had noticed it she gave the matter all her attention, and soon discovered that it had to do with

Longton Place – or at least to going back there. It was not long before Emily, always a good listener, noticed how often Joan brought the conversation round to the church.

Emily had accepted Nannie Ludgrove's rule that one week she took the children to sit with her in the family pew and the next the under nurse took them. The idea was that on the alternate Sunday the one not attending matins should go to the evening service. There was not much of what Emily called churchyfying about the morning service, for whoever was in charge spent their time telling the children not to fidget or, still worse, to talk. Emily seldom got to the evening service for there was always the chance Matthew might have one of his attacks. So, though she knew that owing to the Rector having been ill a young curate was taking the services, she had not given him more than the passing thought that he had a face unusually like a rabbit. Now it became clear to her that to Joan he was very far from looking like a rabbit and that she must find something pleasant to say.

'Have you spoken to that young man who's in charge while Rector's ill?'

It was all Joan needed. Her cheeks burned and her eyes shone. She had indeed spoken to him. She had done more, she had been seeing him regularly. He was staying at the Rectory and after evening church they always had a nice little talk.

But Emily missed the rest. It had never crossed her mind

that Joan might marry, and now that there was a possibility it was not of Joan she was thinking but of her nurslings. The schoolroom worked splendidly as they were. The last thing she wanted was a change. For only God knew what they might get. Someone fresh like enough, certain to be someone with new-fangled ways. She was glad to find that conversations about her curate were easy to carry on with Joan who expected little in response.

'Just like one of the children,' Emily thought. In the pauses she said 'You don't give to get' or 'It'll all be Sir Garnet' or some other of Nannie Ludgrove's saws. When it was clear that even Joan had no more to say she folded her work and, speaking just as she would to one of the children, observed: 'Well, dear, time for Bedfordshire.'

When the snow came to an end Emily had another shock. While the freeze lasted the men servants were constantly out with trays of hot drinks, and this had suited Alice who had an eye for the boys. She being with the children there was no getting together, but there were many enquiries about her time off. As a result Alice told Emily she wanted a change.

'I'm sorry, Nannie, truly I am, but time is passing and I would like to better myself. I'd like a place where there was more life – footmen and that.'

The end of the cold spell brought Miss Jane and Master Timothy to the nursery. Miss Jane was exquisitely pretty and shortly being taken to France to live with a French family for a year. Master Timothy was at Eton. With them came Miss Ursula and Master Stephen now eleven and nine. They gathered round the nursery table where all kinds of card games were played. In these Henry and Mary were allowed to join. The noise was terrific.

'Isn't it nice here now Nannie Etheridge has gone?' Miss Jane said. 'Do you remember how she wouldn't let us talk?'

'And how she beat us with her hair brush, the old pig.' Master Timothy caught Emily's eye and gave his lion growl. Emily, sewing by the fire, did not care for that kind of talk.

'That's enough,' she said gently. 'Least said, soonest mended.'

'I would have thought it should be most said soonest punished,' Henry suggested.

Thomas was considered too small for card games but he held his own in that conversation.

'Judge not, that ye be not judged.'

There was a slight pause while all at the table took in what he had said. Then Thomas was rewarded with an enormous laugh. Questions were fired at him.

'Where did you hear that?'

'Is it from the Bible?'

'Can you quote other things?'

Emily watched Thomas. He appeared uninterested but she knew he was secretly loving his seconds in the limelight. For a moment she longed to do what her mother would have done, given Thomas a slap saying, 'That's no way to speak Bible or some such.' Instead she spoke to Jane:

'Go on with your game, dear. Master Thomas is not to blame, he quotes like a little parrot. He does not know how silly it makes him sound.'

But that night when she said her prayers she asked for help with Thomas. 'I don't like to scold him, he's little more than a baby, but he's a show-off which I don't hold with in my nursery, so please help me, God.' She swallowed and copied Lady Reeve: 'Gawd, I should say.'

As things turned out Emily lost both Joan and Alice at the same time. Lady Reeve came to stay and because she, Emily, was her protégée she told her about Joan's feelings for the curate. Lady Reeve was cautious at first. The clergy were often younger sons of the aristocracy, in which case Joan would not do. But if this young man proved to be of humbler stock then Joan might suit him very well. She had been given a good education and both she and her mama knew their place. It would be, of course, a feather in Mrs Bun's cap if her daughter married into the church and it was certainly worth looking into.

When, in later years, Emily talked of Joan it did not sound as if the curate had much to do with his own marriage. Lady Reeve had spoken to him and arranged for Sylvia to invite him to the house. It was then learned that he had no blue blood, his father being a dentist, at that date not received socially. But even baronets have to have their teeth attended to, and it was during a series of well-carried-out dental work that the Baronet heard the story of the dentist's eldest son, whose name was Albert, who was insisting he wished to take Holy Orders. There were many incumbencies in his Baronet's gift, it was therefore a matter of one letter to arrange as soon as the young man was ordained deacon to place him as curate to some man to whom he had given a living, but who was getting on in years, and would be glad of help.

As for Alice, there was no difficulty at all, she had worked well so Mrs Smith would give her a good reference and was sure a suitable place could be found for her.

It was a quiet wedding from Joan's home but greatly honoured for Mary, wearing white with a wide, pink sash, stayed with her grandmama in order to be bridesmaid. Lady Reeve, who brought Mary back, told Emily the wedding had passed very pleasantly.

'Miss Mary showed good training for she never fidgeted once.'

Alice had been taken to look after Mary – 'says it was ever so pretty'.

'It was Gawd's will,' said Lady Reeve.

Even Emily, who seldom had such thoughts, was surprised

at this. She considered the wedding owed everything to her Ladyship.

Lady Reeve stayed on to interview governesses. The plan was to find a French woman but in this she failed. What she wanted – and indeed most ladies wanted – was somebody who had worked for a friend. In the end they had to fall back on an agency, something Lady Reeve gravely mistrusted, for she had always instructed Mrs Honeysett to engage her staff from families living on the estate or recommendations from friends or relations. However, a governess had to be found and quickly for otherwise Sylvia could see she would again be expected to teach.

'Let us have a night in London,' she suggested to her mother, 'and visit the agencies together.'

The agency, to Lady Reeve's surprise, proved to be a most respectable place with an owner who knew how to treat her superiors. There were three governesses waiting to be interviewed. The first they saw was hopeless, a giggling young thing who scarcely seemed able to read, but the other two were both admirable and well qualified. They could, besides the usual subjects, teach painting and drawing and the rudiments of piano playing. Both were found, when tested, to speak French with a tolerable accent. Both belonged to the Church of England. Where the young women differed was in their outlook. Selina Goodley was gentle, perhaps a trifle humble. Miss Lettuce Hanley was a stronger character, reserved, for she never answered more than was necessary but with an eagerness about her that was pleasing. It was her first place but her two references could not be bettered, both were from members of the aristocracy. When the girls had been interviewed Lady Reeve and Sylvia looked at each other, quite unable to decide.

'The person we want now is Nannie,' said Lady Reeve. 'She would know at once which we should have.'

Sylvia knew what she and Tom would have done. She had a card in her reticule. She tore it in half, then on one piece she wrote L.H. and on the other S.G. She shuffled them and laid them face down on her lap.

'Pick one, Mama.'

To Lady Reeve this savoured of gambling so was not to be approved of; luck should play no part in so serious a matter.

'Let us pray to Gawd to advise us,' she suggested.

'Do,' Sylvia agreed, 'and then draw.'

A minute later Lady Reeve turned over a piece of card. On it was written L.H.

Lettuce had not had an easy life. She had never known her mother or her father. She guessed that her father had not belonged to her mother's world, for he did not appear in what little of her history she knew. Her mother, with her own old

Nannie, had been sent to France where they had lived quietly until the baby was born. There had been a christening somewhere for the baby was given two godmothers, both the daughters of Earls, and both were appointed her guardians. She and her Nannie were then settled in a private wing of a house in Essex. Lettuce presumed, from what happened later, that what appeared an adequate income was settled on her. But the two daughters of Earls knew nothing about husbanding money, so had Lettuce brought up as they had been themselves. There were expensive clothes and a pony and trap and, when she was ready for it, a good school. There were not many schools at that date so they sent her to Cheltenham. This worked well for she was a clever child, but in her early teens the money settled on her came to an end, and without warning her godmothers appeared to say she must leave school and earn her own living. Cheltenham came to the rescue, appointing her a pupil teacher, which Lettuce found humiliating. However, she stuck it out until she was old enough to work. The godmothers wrote her references and Lettuce put her name down at an agency, to be subsequently selected by the turn of a card to go to Longton Place.

Before Lettuce arrived Emily found an under nurse and a nursery maid. Sisters called Polly and Annie, country girls, daughters of a dairyman. Polly had been kept at home because her mother had died when she was twelve and there were five others besides Annie to be brought up. Then, when she was eighteen and Annie twelve, her father had married again, so Polly had decided to find a place in a good nursery. As it happened Mrs Smith had connections with the village where Polly lived and when, in a roundabout way, the news reached her that there was a nice girl looking for a nursery situation she told Emily. Emily sent for Polly, to whom she at once took, and hearing of the other children at home told her she could send for Annie. 'If you brought her up,' Emily said 'I know where I am. We'll soon have her into my ways.'

When Lettuce was due to arrive Mrs Smith, on the principle that one good turn deserves another, went to the nursery.

'There's this new governess coming, could you manage nursery lunch for all? The mistress won't have it though I've tried to tell her, but things are changing, staff won't work as they did, always wanting time off and that, and when they go out dressed you can't tell who's who. It's not what I'm used to. So if you could see your way to nursery lunch for all it would be a help.'

Emily never answered in a hurry.

'I'll think it over and let you know.'

Emily knew it would be managed. A little crowded but Lucy's chair could be beside her at the top of the table, and it would mean there would be no talk of schoolroom meals for Matthew when the time came. He was best kept under her eye. Then there was Thomas, she would see he didn't get above himself. He would need quietening down after a morning spent showing off to Miss Hanley.

Though Emily had no idea of it there was anxiety felt by many as to how Nannie would get on with the new governess.

To make quite sure that all went smoothly Lady Reeve came to stay for a week while Lettuce settled in. Lettuce was amused at her anxiety over the schoolroom. 'Surely,' she thought, 'nothing very elaborate is wanted for little children all under seven.'

However, when she met the children she felt differently. Henry was such a very brilliant seven-year-old. It was true she was not to teach him for long as he was to join his brother at school in the autumn, but it was difficult at first to work out a scheme of teaching which included hearing Henry dash through a chapter of the Bible and teaching Matthew his alphabet. Then there was Mary who was supposed to have a daily piano lesson and, finally, glib little Thomas storing up unwanted information like a squirrel storing nuts. To Lady Reeve's anxious enquiries as to how the lessons had gone she said cheerfully she might have to re-arrange the room. Planning lessons for four children of such different attainments needed thought. There was not a suggestion of a bob or of a M'Lady and Lady Reeve did not mind. Gawd had chosen Lettuce and anyway, when you remember her references! She was however more worried about the meal arrangements.

'I wonder if that is wise,' she said to Sylvia when she learned that there were to be no school meals. 'It is so important she should get on with Nannie. I had thought, to begin with, you might do better to keep them apart.'

Lettuce's Nannie was by then an old woman but, in all other respects, so like Emily that it was all Lettuce could do not to give her a hug. Everything she said and did was what her own Nannie would say or do. Brought up entirely by a Nannie with no relatives and no friends – for her Nannie had not allowed her to talk to the village children – she knew all there was to know about correct nursery behaviour, and she listened with nostalgia as the familiar nursery sayings dropped softly from Emily's mouth.

'Now, Miss Mary, remember those that leave their potatoes get no pudding.'

And when Mary retorted: 'I don't care, Nannie,' equally softly Nannie replied:

'Don't care was made to care. Don't care lost a duck.'

How often she had heard that in relation to root vegetables. Or when the pudding was finished, that day a blancmange, how well she knew she would hear:

'Now, dears, no scraping. We always leave something for Mr Manners.'

Almost that first day it was accepted without anything

being said that Lettuce was welcome in the nursery or on the afternoon nursery walk, whenever she chose to join them.

Polly and Annie settled happily into nursery ways. They were real country girls with hearty appetites and an easy acceptance of life as it was, with no particular wish to improve their lot. Annie, a big girl for twelve, happily carried up the nursery meals, for she enjoyed her glimpses of kitchen life.

'I really think everything is running splendidly,' Lady Reeve said to Sylvia on one of her visits. 'We have much for which to thank Gawd.'

In May Tom came home. That evening Emily came down with the children after tea. This was partly to be sure the children recognised their father and partly to welcome him home.

'The mistress says he won't be dressed as a soldier which is a pity, they'd like to see him dressed up.'

Lady Reeve, as a suitable welcoming touch, had provided sailor suits for the boys and a sailor blouse with a skirt for Mary.

'You look like an Admiral with your crew,' Lettuce, who had come up to see the new clothes, said admiringly.

'Pity John couldn't be home,' said Nannie. 'There was talk of it.'

'I expect his father will go down and see him at school,' Lettuce suggested.

Nannie shook her head.

'Not if I know my Miss Sylvia. Now she's got him home, she'll not let him out of her sight again.'

It must have been a charming picture, the children dressed as sailors greeting their sunburnt papa safe home from the war. In actual fact, as Emily remembered in later years, it was not altogether a happy reunion. Henry hung back.

'You see, Nannie,' he told her afterwards, 'I couldn't remember if we kissed or shook hands.'

Little Lucy, Emily thought, screamed when he came near her. 'You know how babies sometimes are with strangers,' she would say, 'Matthew hung on to my apron. Thomas was the one, of course, saluting and carrying on. But what made the master feel welcome was Mary. I don't know if she remembered him but she never was shy, and she ran up to him and hugged him round the waist and he picked her up and kissed her, and, as I remember, it made me want to cry for the look on his face. I suppose, like most fathers, he would cut off his hands for his little girls.'

That summer they went to The Hall again. Emily tried to arrange for Polly and Annie to have a week's holiday each but the girls refused.

'Maybe you could give us time off,' Polly suggested. 'We don't want to go home. There's nought there for us, I ran cottage my way and she runs it hers, we wouldn't never agree.'

'But Annie then, wouldn't she like a week at home?'

Polly gave a pleasant, earthy smile.

'Annie is counting on stayin' at Hall. She has heard of the men servants around.'

Emily always laughed when she told this. For Polly and Annie had both married servants from The Hall, 'but had led them a wonderful dance before they was caught'.

It was taken for granted by Emily and by Lady Reeve that Lettuce would be going home for her holiday. She had given as her address when she came to work at Longton Place the cottage which was her Nannie's. It was in a village near the one in which she had been brought up. But her Nannie was getting very old and could neither see nor hear as she had done, so there was talk of her moving in with relations who would take care of her. This meant that Lettuce had no home outside Longton Place.

Nannie and Lettuce were together in the nursery when the subject of Lettuce's holiday was mentioned. Emily was packing and Lettuce was giving her a hand. With pride Nannie showed Lettuce the little French boots and Brotherly Love.

'When the place is right, all the elder ones take turns with Brotherly Love, but they none of them have fitted into the boots.'

Lettuce was amused.

'Then why pack them?'

'Because of what was said by the wonderful Nannie who

was here when I first came. You know how it is, servants look down on families who are not so comfortable as some. "Well," she said, "never make a poor mouth." And I never have. Every night, wherever we stay, those beautiful little boots are taken down to the boot-boy to be cleaned.'

'Never make a poor mouth,' thought Lettuce, 'keep your pride even when you've very little to be proud of.

'At my school,' she said, 'I had a head-mistress who said something like that to me.' She took a deep breath and, for the first time, admitted to the unspeakable. 'You see, I'm illegitimate.'

Emily thought nothing of that. In Easden any girl who walked out regularly with a boy took it for granted he would only marry her at the last minute. No bride ever reached the altar without obviously carrying her groom's baby. She was, however, surprised it should have happened to Lettuce, for the gentry did not do things that way, their daughters did not know what love was all about until their wedding night.

'So you have not got a real home to go to.'

Lettuce, having started, was glad to confide in Emily.

'Nowhere. You see, my Nannie brought me up. She came with my mother to France and ... '

Emily let her run on, feeling the out-pouring was doing Lettuce good. Then she asked:

'And your Nannie never told you what your real name was?'

'No never. She knew but she wouldn't say. She loved my mother and a promise is a promise.'

'Where'd your name come from then?'

'I have no idea. I suppose my godmothers chose it when I was old enough to go to school.'

'Godparents had you?'

'Yes. Friends of my mother I suppose. Both are the daughters of Earls.'

'Could you stay with one of them for your holiday?'

'Oh no!' said Lettuce, appalled at the thought. 'I hate them. It was their fault my money did not last. Do you know, all the time I was at school they never wrote. I used to creep out and post post-cards to myself.'

'You come with us to The Hall then,' Emily said. 'There's no time to write but I will find something to say to Miss Sylvia. You will have a nice time there, it's a lovely place.'

John came home the day before the family left for The Hall. Tom had not been able to go down to the school to see him. In fact he had not been able to go away anywhere for he found his affairs in a sad muddle. He had left a bailiff in charge of farm matters, a young man who seemed 'bettermost' as they said locally, but he lacked authority. He did at first run to Sylvia with his problems but soon learned there was no help to be had there. So cottages needed repairing and the land was starved by bad husbandry.

'I'll have my nose to the grindstone from now till next

year,' he told Sylvia when she pleaded with him to go visiting.

Sylvia pouted but she knew she was partly to blame and anyway it was so good to have Tom home, even if he would spend his days riding round the estate. Then, praise be to God, there were to be no more babies, the doctor had talked to Tom about that.

'Don't be cross with naughty me,' she would say. 'I never did know about farms.'

Actually Tom had planned to drive to the station to meet John. It was pure bad luck that a meeting of landowners called him away.

John was looking forward to seeing his father but it was not of him he was thinking when the dog-cart stopped at the front door. Without saying a word he was out of the dog-cart and flying through the house, up the nursery stairs, through the little nursery gate and into Emily's arms. She was alone for the children were out with Polly and Annie.

'My boy!' she whispered, 'my own dear boy.' Then, putting him away from her so that she could see him, she caught her breath. 'Why, you've got a black eye.'

John thought nothing of a black eye.

'It'll go. Where are the others?'

'Out walking. You're earlier than expected. Have you seen your mama?'

John dismissed that. 'I'll go down presently. I wish we weren't going away tomorrow, there's so much I want to see here. How is everybody?'

'All well, thank God, even Matthew. He hasn't had one of his bad turns in weeks.'

Tom, coming home from his meeting, flung open the drawing-room door expecting to see John.

'Where is he?' he asked Sylvia.

She pouted.

'With Nannie of course. You would think at his age he was too old for a nursery and you know how simple Nannie is, he can't talk to her.'

Tom was fond of Emily but had accepted Sylvia was not.

'He'll be down in a minute,' he said mildly. 'I expect he has scars to show Nannie he won't show us.'

So when a few minutes later John arrived he was quite pleased with the black eye.

'What did Nannie have to say about that? Who gave it to you?'

'A boy called Elliot.'

'I hope you gave him one back.'

John was surprised.

'Why should I? I like him.'

Tom was shocked. Of course schoolboys got black eyes, but it was the rule you gave not only as good as you got but better if you could manage it.

What had he given birth to? He must take John in hand these holidays, he had been away too long.

At The Hall Mrs Honeysett had news for Emily. She invited her down after supper and gave her a glass of parsnip wine.

'Lottie, my parlourmaid, is leaving,' she sniffed, 'to better herself, she says, but I think she's set her cap at the publican near her home. Anyway, be that as it may, I remembered my promise so I have written to your mother offering the place to your sister if she should suit. She will be here before you leave.'

Emily saw herself walking beside Betty to her first place, a funny little figure with her hair screwed up under a cheap straw hat. As she walked she had kept tripping over her first long dress and her Sunday coat. Would it be like that for Sarah? Emily tried to feel pleased at Mrs Honeysett's kindness but she did not feel easy. Her father's words were still in her ears: 'Sarah will need a middlin' bunt if she don't mend her ways.' What ways? She hoped all her father had meant was that Sarah, as the only girl, had missed a few healthy smacks when Betty was handing them out, so might be the better for them now.

Tom had a talk with the Baronet about John. Telling him what John had said about his black eye. The Baronet was startled.

'Looks manly enough to me, doesn't write poetry or such nonsense, does he?'

Tom was disgusted at the idea.

'Nothing like that. Gets good reports from Tomkins. Manly enough as far as I know. Joins in everything that's goin' on. Got a good seat on a horse.'

The Baronet beckoned to Tom to come nearer. He dropped his voice.

'Your mother-in-law is a splendid woman, none finer, but maybe a bit too fond of Bible reading. All right for girls but you don't want too much for boys, not healthy. I wonder if she got at John. All that turning the other cheek stuff.'

Tom said hesitantly: 'Sylvia is of course a wonderful girl but . . .'

The Baronet dismissed Sylvia with a loving smile.

'Sylvia, bless her, has straw where her brain ought to be, always had. Don't care for Nannie. She doesn't know when she's well off. Send John out with old Butterwell, my head gamekeeper. Spends all day killing things, he'll come back covered in blood, that ought to toughen him.'

John went out with Butterwell, a dear old man who, for all the bodies of stoats, weasels and other such which were hung up round the sheds where he bred his game-birds, took no pleasure in killing. Nor had he any wish to catch poachers.

'I must, when they takes Sir's birds,' he told John, 'but rabbits is for all. I don't see a poacher if all he has on him is a rabbit.'

What John and Butterwell struck up was a friendship over wild flowers. It was a pleasure to the old man to show John his treasures, a rare orchid or an unusual water plant. The only difficulty was that Butterwell called many flowers by the same name: Jack by the Hedge was his name for both wild garlic and red campion. He thought John seemed a fine boy and so he told the Baronet.

'Puts me in mind of you, young John does.'

The Baronet told Tom he thought he was barking up the wrong tree. 'Old Butterwell likes the boy.'

It was that summer that Emily met Dick, a gipsyish-looking young man with unusually green fingers. He had worked his way up and had come to The Hall as second gardener.

The Baronet was fond of travel and usually went abroad during the winter months. He would return with his pockets full of seeds, which Dick took to his special shed and usually succeeded in rearing. One morning, when Emily came out into the garden with Matthew and Lucy, the Baronet and Dick were bent over a plant. Hearing the children, the Baronet straightened up.

'Look here, Nannie, you're fond of flowers. Came back with some seeds a year ago and look how this fellow has brought them on. Have you met him? His name is Dick but it ought to be green fingers.'

Dick touched his cap to the children then he beamed at Emily.

'I seen you most days but distant.'

Emily had never been one for boys, her nursery was her life, but there was something about Dick. Suddenly her world shifted a little. The grass was greener, the flower scents stronger, the sun hotter. There was a honeysuckle climbing over a summerhouse. All her life she connected the smell of honeysuckle with Dick.

Back in the nursery getting Lucy ready for luncheon Polly gave Emily a thoughtful look.

'You been and lost a penny and picked up a sixpence?'

Emily smiled a slow, dreamy smile.

'Me. Why?'

'You look like it, that's why.'

From that day on, no matter where Emily took the children they always ran into Dick. They did not talk much, sometimes no more than exchange greetings. However little was said every word was treasured and later thought over and wondered about. Then one day the nursery party were caught in a heavy shower of rain. Lucy was all right for there was a hood to the baby carriage, but Matthew had no protection at all from the storm. Matthew ran for shelter under some trees and Emily half ran, half walked pushing

Lucy behind him. But before they reached the trees Dick appeared and swept Matthew into his arms.

'Follow me, Mrs Huckwell,' he said, 'my hut is quite near.'

It was only afterwards Emily wondered where he had learned her name. Nobody called her Mrs Huckwell. Imagine!

The hut was really more of a greenhouse. All round there were shelves on which stood boxes full of growing seeds. The roof had glass windows which Dick gently closed. He found a box for Emily to sit on and a bit of towel and carefully dried Matthew.

'Now you have a look round, Master Matthew. Queer old seeds many of these be.'

Only one person heard a first-hand account of that first meeting and that, many years later, was Lucy. Between Emily and Dick there was never any doubt it was love at first sight. Emily, never one to find words easily, said that Dick's hut that morning seemed to be filled with a golden light. Considering how hard it was raining at the time this was a great flight of imagination.

Dick told Emily about where he lived.

'Rightly I should have a cottage being second gardener, but not being married I couldn't manage like, so I bide along of the head gardener, Mr Binstead. He be getting on Mr Binstead do be but he's still a rare gardener, but he suffers the rheumatics cruel though he always carries a potato in his pocket.'

'Were you born in these parts?' Emily asked.

'No, my father were a traveller but not my mother and she never wanted travelling for me, so she sent me to her brother who was a gardener. He treated me hard but he learned me.'

Presently the rain thinned and a weak sun tried to shine.

'Better move,' said Dick, 'it still looks rainified.'

Emily pushed the baby carriage out of the shed and called to Matthew. Then outside they saw a wonderful thing – a great rainbow stretching over them.

Ten days before they left for home Sarah arrived. Mrs Honeysett had warned Emily she was coming so Emily sent her a message to tell her to come up and see her when she was free, for she remembered how lonely and homesick she had felt when starting in her first place. Mrs Honeysett spoke to Emily when she took the children out for their morning walk.

'It's early days yet. No one would guess she was your sister. Nothing bold about you.'

Mrs Honeysett moved on then so Emily had no chance to ask what she meant by 'bold'. On the whole though perhaps it was best not to ask for she thought she knew the answer.

*

The next day Sarah came up to the nursery after tea. She looked charming in her black afternoon dress, white cap and apron and was much more friendly and easy to talk to than she was at home. She was, Emily suspected, rather over-awed by everything.

'The meals!' she said. 'I never saw so much food, of course you hardly ate in the servants' hall but you ought to see the goings-on. We all have our proper places to sit and then Mr Johnstone says grace and then he carves the joint, but you ought to see what happens after. Mr Johnstone leads out the heads, then the visiting valets and ladies maids, each carrying their glass of water in one hand and their bread in the other, troop after him to Mrs Honeysett's room where their pudding is served.'

Emily knew this strange arrangement went on though she had no part in it.

'I could not get down for prayers this morning. Where do you sit for that?'

'Next to the first parlourmaid. She says I follow her in to church on Sundays, but she follows me out as we have to form up outside to bob when the family comes out.'

'What do you do in the evenings?' Emily asked. 'You can always come up here, only of course we are leaving in a few days.'

A smile slid across Sarah's face.

'No, thank you. The evenings are fun, we play cards and

that. We do what we like seemingly if we don't make too much noise, for the heads all stay in Pug's Parlour, as they call Mrs Honeysett's room.'

Emily did not want to be the nagging sister but Sarah was still very young.

'Well, take care of yourself and try and get to bed early for you need your sleep.'

Emily had one other short talk with Mrs Honeysett before she left. It was after church on their last Sunday.

'I think your sister is settling down.'

Emily was grateful.

'Oh, thank you. I do hope she suits.'

Before they returned to Longton Place a ceremony had to be performed called 'saying goodbye to Granny'. The children visited her separately each carrying their Bible. Lady Reeve was not always in the same room for this occasion. That year she was in her conservatory. This was a glasshouse leading out of the drawing-room, it was always full of flowers for it was under Mr Binstead's special care. In the centre of the conservatory was a stone figure of a boy riding on a dolphin and when a button was pressed a pump worked and water sprayed out of the dolphin's mouth. The boy had originally been naked but Lady Reeve had hired a local craftsman who had shrouded the boy in a kind of metal tunic.

Each child, as they visited their grandmother, had to read

that portion of the Bible chosen for the day and, if asked, discuss it afterwards. That day the Bible reading was from *John*, Chapter Six. The story of the miracle of the loaves and fishes. John, with his finger in his Bible to keep the place, stood in front of his grandmother. She was sitting under an exotic plant, her hair as usual covered by a lace cap. As much as was possible Lady Reeve avoided the ostentation and opulence of the clothes of the period. Some things she could not escape. Her figure, thanks largely to her corsets, was shaped like an 'S', as were the figures of all ladies at that date and often of their staff too. 'Lamentable but true' Lady Reeve had said when her attention was drawn to this. 'It spells disaster when young women forget their place.' That morning her black dress – the country was still in mourning for Queen Victoria – had just sufficient lace dripping from it to keep her in fashion, and her neck was encased in a black lace, boned collar. Lettuce, who had been ordered to bring the children to the 'saying goodbye to grandmother' ceremony, thought it was lucky the children were fond of their grandmother for to her she was rather an alarming figure.

John, having kissed his grandmother, opened his Bible and started to read. He read clearly and distinctly to the end of verse 13.

'Very good, dear,' said Lady Reeve. 'Now tell me what food the lad had in his basket.'

'Five barley loaves and two small fishes.'

Lady Reeve smiled, then she handed him a gold sovereign and a piece of barley sugar of the type she always had by her, square lumps hanging on a string.

As John left the conservatory Henry came in. Henry could read beautifully and that day, much to Lettuce's relief, he did. But his grandmother checked that he had taken in what he read.

'What food did the lad carry that Jesus used for this miracle?'

Henry tried to remember what was in the boy's basket.

'Loaves and fishes,' he suggested.

'How many loaves and how many fishes and of what were the loaves made?'

Henry did not know so he was sent away without a prize to study further what he had read.

'Come back after Lucy has said her little prayer.'

After Henry had gone out Lady Reeve beckoned to Lettuce.

'You heard that. Now, do not forget to do the same when you are hearing the children read the Bible. Question, question, question. No child of my family must read like a parrot.'

Mary came in looking, Lady Reeve thought, charming in a blue frock with the rather long skirts then in fashion for little girls. She was really a remarkably pretty child, thought her grandmother complacently. Mary opened her book and clearly and slowly read the verses exactly as Lettuce had taught her. She was ready with her answer if Granny asked a question. Henry had whispered the question to her as he came out of the drawing-room. Having finished reading she closed her Bible and looked expectantly at her grandmother. She did not want the gold piece for that was taken from her and saved, but she did want her lump of barley sugar.

'In the story you have just read so nicely, how many people sat down to eat?'

Mary had her lips open to say 'five barley loaves' but she closed them abruptly. This was cheating, why was she being asked a different question to Henry? What John was asked didn't count for he always knew all Bible answers. How many people sat down to eat? She had just read it, why didn't she know the answer?

'You don't know, do you, Mary?' said Lady Reeve sadly. 'That means you are reading like a little parrot. You were not thinking about what you were reading.'

Mary was furious, she stamped, she threw her Bible at her grandmother, she lay on the floor and screamed. Lady Reeve signalled to Lettuce to do nothing. Without attention Mary's temper soon wore out. She sat up and smiled shamefacedly at her grandmother.

'I thought it was not right to ask me that, I know everything else.'

Lady Reeve pointed to the Bible.

'Pick it up. I cannot forgive you for throwing a Bible about, that is a sin which only Gawd can forgive.'

Mary always felt good after an attack of temper.

'That will be all right. God knows about my temper. Every day I ask him to make it better. I think he's trying but I suppose he's got a lot else to do.'

'We must help to cure that temper,' said Lady Reeve. 'I will send Miss Hanley something you are to learn by heart.'

Mary stood up and shook out her skirts. She looked longingly at the box of barley sugar.

'I know I was bad so I can't have my gold piece, but do you think perhaps a very small piece of barley sugar?'

Lady Reeve's lips twitched. She studied the barley sugar in the box and found a small piece which she gave to Mary.

'You may have this little piece but remember what a temper may lead to. There are men and women hanged every day for murder, many of whom would not have committed their terrible crimes had they not lost their tempers.'

That year Henry went with John to Mr Tomkins' school. He too, was provided with a tuck-box made on the estate and a selection of good things to pack in it arrived from his grandfather. Emily always found plenty to do but the nursery was now empty for part of the morning, for even

Lucy went down for early lessons. What Mary was to learn to cure her temper had arrived from her grandmother. It was written in large letters mounted on cardboard, like a text to hang on a wall. It came, as Lettuce at once recognised, from Katherine's speech in 'The Taming of the Shrew'.

'A woman mov'd is like a fountain troubled,
Muddy, ill-seeming, thick, bereft of beauty;
And while it is so, none so dry or thirsty
Will deign to sip, or touch one drop of it.'

Lettuce unwillingly accepted the inevitable.

'You must learn this by heart, Mary, and I will explain to you what each word means. Then we will hang it over your bed.'

Mary was a quick learner but she found those words hard going, and she had to keep at it for no one knew when Lady Reeve might turn up.

Emily found herself longing for news of any sort from The Hall. She could not expect Dick to write, his father having been a traveller it was doubtful if he could, anyway not more than he needed for his gardening. Come to that, she wasn't much of a hand at letter writing herself. But she thought about Dick a lot and remembered all he had said. Particularly she remembered how, one day when he had met her out walking with Lucy, he had talked of the cottage he would have when he was wed. The flowers he would grow and the chickens he would raise. 'If there is one thing I do love it is baby chicks running about a flower bed.' Emily thought about this so often that almost she could feel the softness of a baby chick in her hands.

When they had first come home from The Hall, although Dick filled her thoughts when she was alone, she had not even considered the possibility of marriage. She could not see the day when she could leave her children. Matthew needed so much attention and Lucy was still not much more than a baby. But as the months passed things changed. Matthew seemed stronger and Lucy was getting to the stage when she hated her hand held even on stairs. She really no longer needed both Polly and Annie. Was the day coming when the mistress would say she no longer needed her? Once that would have been unthinkable but now there was a wonderful alternative, an alternative that would not cut her off from her nurslings, for they would of course still visit their grandparents.

Very occasionally Emily had a short letter from Sarah. Sarah was evidently doing well at The Hall. The Reeves had several children, all of whom were married, who came to stay. There were any number of cousins the Burton children had never met. It seemed that the elder cousins were growing up and Sarah was ordered to maid the young ladies.

'Ever so sweet they are and full of fun and so are the young gentlemen. There are younger ones but I don't see them of course ... '

Once she mentioned a Lady Rose: 'Her father is an Earl and they live in Ireland, she is very pretty and full of fun, she has given me two dresses. I wish when she marries I could work for her as her own maid.'

Alas for Sarah, Emily had a curt note from Mrs Honeysett to say that Sarah had proved unsuitable so had been sent home. Emily was sorry but, she thought to herself, Sarah would get another place. The truth was Emily had another worry on her mind. It was Thomas. Next year he was to go to school. Naturally she knew he was going, and it should not have worried her, for clever Thomas was just the boy to slip into school life as if he were born to it. But lately, for one reason or another, he was always on her mind.

Then Lettuce spoke about him. She came to the nursery for that purpose.

'I'm not happy about Thomas.'

'If only,' thought Emily, 'she had not put it like that she could have pushed what she had said aside and changed the subject.' But Thomas was one of her boys, one of her children whom she had carried in her arms.

'What has Thomas done?'

'I thought at first it was just that he is used to being the clever one but now I do not know. But twice lately he's been through my books.'

Emily let the sewing she was doing fall into her lap.

'Why would he do that?'

'It's sums. He's not so clever at figures. The answers are printed in the book. He's been copying the answers.'

'What makes you think that?'

'I suppose he was in a hurry for he did not put the book back where I keep it.'

'I suppose in his child's way he thinks he's getting ready for school.'

'That's what I am afraid of. If he thinks he has always to be the clever one, no matter how he does it, he'll be beaten at school or he could be sent home.'

Emily knew she must say what she did not want to say.

'I'm afraid he sometimes takes what is not his. Last time we went out to tea there was a little gun come back with us. I took it to the mistress and said Lucy must have picked it up. But I knew.'

Lettuce said:

'Then he takes fruit when it's ripe. Gets it from the glasshouses or off the kitchen garden wall.'

Emily smiled.

'All the children do that. They know they must not but it's for devilment.'

Lettuce shook her head.

'With Thomas it's different somehow. Besides, I do not think he would stop at fruit. He has always got to be Master Clever and, if he wanted something enough, I think he would take it. That day you kept him indoors last week with a cold. Well, when I was out with Mary, he went to my room.'

Emily gasped.

'Whatever would he do that for?'

'I do not know. I caught him coming out. He had this in his hand.'

Lettuce passed Emily a card. It was an Easter card with a cross drawn on it and 'He is risen' written under it. Emily turned it over, on the reverse side was written 'Love from Nannie'.

'What would he take that for?'

Lettuce shook her head.

'I cannot imagine. I use it as a marker in my prayer book. He could have seen it in church. I daresay he used it to prove he really had been in my room. None of what he does is important but altogether it frightens me. He is so different from the others. Do you think a child can be born bad, Nannie?'

Of course there were black sheep in families, even in the best families, it got talked about in servants' halls. Mostly that kind got sent abroad somewhere. Had it shown when they were children? Emily had never heard but perhaps it had.

'I do not know, dear.' Emily looked at Lettuce. 'Was there something you thought I could do?'

'No. It's what I have to do. I am going to talk to his father.'

'And tell him what?'

'That he is past learning from me and could he get the school to take him next term. They do take some at seven, John told me.'

Emily was afraid for Thomas.

'You would not think he would be better here where we can keep an eye on him?'

Lettuce shook her head.

'No. I am sure school is what he needs and the sooner the better.'

What exactly Lettuce said to Tom Emily never knew for Lettuce kept it to herself. In fact it was not Lettuce who told Emily the result of her talk. Tom joined her when she was out in the grounds with Matthew and Lucy. The children ran to their father each clutching a hand. Tom gave them both a gentle push.

'Run along for a minute. I want a word with Nannie.' He waited until they were out of earshot then he said: 'Miss Hanley says Thomas is too clever for her. She wants me to ask the school to take him next term. I can't understand this for Mr Tomkins has written to me to say how well Henry has settled down and how exceptionally well he has been taught. Thomas has always been a sharp child but does he seem to you old enough for school?'

There was a pause then Emily said:

'I think if Miss Hanley says he will do better at school, sir, then she will be right. He has never been what I would call a nursery boy.'

The family went to The Hall for Christmas and at once it was realised in the nursery that there were secrets in the air. For, as was well known in every nursery, 'little pitchers have long ears'.

'And it's not to do with Christmas,' said Mary, 'nor with you going to school next term, Thomas. It's something quite separate and I don't think it happens yet.'

'Why not yet?' asked Thomas, annoyed. Mary had news – if she had – before he had it.

'Well,' Mary admitted, 'this is really a guess but Grandmama said to Mama she thought mine should have pink under it and yours, Lucy, should have blue, and we should have hats to match. They were whispering so that's all I heard.'

'Sounds like a summer thing,' said Matthew.

'That's what I think,' Mary agreed.

'I think we should all try and find out,' Matthew suggested.

'We'll have to be very careful nobody knows we're finding out,' Thomas said. 'You know how grown-ups are, they keep things secret in case we get over-excited and Matthew has his asthma.'

'John and Henry will be coming here tomorrow,' said Mary. 'I would think Henry would find out, he's a very good finder-outer.'

John and Henry reached The Hall the next afternoon. As usual, John raced up to the nursery and this time there was Henry to follow him, and Emily was hugged by both of them at once.

'Can we have tea with you?' the boys asked.

Emily, all aglow because her two boys were home, looked fondly at John.

'I told your mama I thought you would be hungry after your journey. Those little scraps of things Mr Johnstone serves the drawing-room wouldn't do. So it's tea up here with boiled eggs.'

'And honey?' Henry asked. 'We never get honey at school.'

'And honey,' Emily agreed.

Perhaps because they were at The Hall and, if only it would clear – it had rained since they arrived – Emily would see Dick next day, she never forgot that tea-party. Matthew was well, a joy in itself, and John and Henry looked splendid, plate after plate of bread and butter disappeared covered with honey, followed by slices of dripping cake. And they would have eaten the table-cloth, Emily thought, if it had not been time to change the younger ones to go down to the drawing-room. Emily tried to get the boys into their Eton suits, which Polly had unpacked, but they would not wear them.

'They won't expect it, first night of the holidays,' said Henry.

Emily did not go down with the children that night. There was no longer a need for anyone to accompany them, but it was the custom and customs die hard so she sent Polly.

Annie came up with her tray and cleared away the tea things, and Emily set her nursery to rights and then got her work-basket. There would be a lot of stitching and darning to do when Polly had finished the unpacking. Whoever was meant to do the sewing at that school was no needler.

It was then John came in. As though he was a small boy again he sat on the rug at Emily's feet and laid his head against her knees.

At first he asked for news of home. Emily had known that, fond though he was of The Hall, he was a home boy and would not want to be away for Christmas. Then suddenly he asked:

'Nannie, why are they sending Thomas to school next term? He wasn't coming until the autumn.'

Emily gave herself time to collect her thoughts. She would not lie but she could not tell the truth.

'It seems he's done all the book learning he can with Miss Hanley. He's that sharp she has to work at her lessons before she gives them to him.'

John had a worried frown.

'I wish they wouldn't send him. He won't like it. There are some of his age but that's because their parents are in India. They mostly horse around, Thomas won't like it a bit. I mean I expect he thinks he will do things with Henry and me but he won't.'

Emily gave his hair a stroke.

'I expect he will settle down. He's a rare one for getting his way is Master Thomas.'

'But at seven he's only a child.'

Emily smiled.

'At eight you were only a child and it broke my heart to see you go. But look at you now. School has done you no harm.'

The next day the sun came out and Emily told Polly she would take Matthew and Lucy for their walk. As was her custom when they were in the home grounds she let the children run ahead. Probably she expected to hear: 'Go' mornin', Miss Lucy, Master Matthew. How you been keeping then?' Soon Emily and Dick were walking together towards a bit of woodland.

'There's a bank there that gets the sun,' Dick told the children, 'and there's some snowdrops is poking through.'

'Can we run on and look, Nannie?' Lucy pleaded.

'You do that,' Emily agreed happily, trying desperately hard to keep her feet from skipping.

Mary had been quite right when she said Henry would find out secrets. One walk with his grandpa and he knew it all.

At the boys' request they had tea every day in the nursery. Though they were warned when guests came at Christmas they must expect to dress up and hand round. After tea Henry drew the others into a corner by the toy cupboard.

'I've found out. But they want to tell you themselves so you must not know.' He paused to be sure he had their attention. 'We're all being taken to London and all the other cousins, the ones we don't know, to see the Coronation.'

'What's that?' asked Lucy.

'When they crown somebody. Before it's always been the Queen, now we're going to have a King and Grandfather has bought a big room with balconies at each window where we can all watch the procession.'

John could see a flaw in this.

'When's this Coronation going to be?'

'June. But it's all right, we are coming home for it.'

'Grandpapa says all schools will send their boys home. There'll be bonfires and fireworks and things.'

'London!' sighed Mary ecstatically. 'How simply perfect! I wish it was June now.'

'But don't forget,' Henry urged, 'it's still a secret. We aren't to know yet because Nannie would say we were over-excited.'

'Or above ourselves,' Mary agreed. 'Now be careful, Lucy, you don't know anything about the Coronation or perhaps they won't let you go.'

The great event was too tremendous to be kept a secret for long. Even for the grown-ups it was wildly exciting. There would be the train journey and then the hotel, and the early start to take their places in the windows. Luncheon would be served afterwards and the Baronet had decided to take Johnstone with them to see to that and, of course, Emily would be there to look after the children.

On Boxing Day, always a quiet, getting-over Christmas Day in country houses, the Baronet announced his news. The children played up splendidly, gasping and clapping their hands, and luckily the Baronet had a lot of extra news to tell – who was coming to the Coronation. *The Times* newspaper almost daily produced extra names: Kings, Princes, Maharajahs, all riding on wonderful horses and all glittering with jewels.

'I am planning this great day,' the Baronet explained, 'because I want June 26 to remain in your memories for ever.'

There were, the children learnt, to be other excitements besides the Coronation itself. There would be parties for all the tenants in every country house. The Government was providing Coronation mugs for all children. There would be decorations as well as bonfires and fireworks. When Emily came to fetch the younger children they were, to her experienced eye, thoroughly over-excited. She collected Lucy from her grandfather's knee and Matthew from his grandmother's lap, and to all protests said gently:

'Come along, dears. Coronation or no Coronation it's time for Bedfordshire.'

Soon after Christmas Emily was invited into Mrs Honeysett's room. She was, Emily could see, ill-at-ease. She gave Emily a glass of her special elderberry wine.

'Very good for keeping the cold out,' she said. Then, when Emily had taken a sip or two, she came to the purpose of her invitation.

'I had to get rid of Sarah. I don't think it was her fault, though she might have led him on, but Lady Rose, whom she was maiding, well, she has a brother. Sarah was seen going into his room.'

Emily, looking upon Sarah as a child, was puzzled what the fuss was about.

'Maybe she took him a message.'

Mrs Honeysett tried not to sound scornful.

'Message! No, dear, your sister is not like you. She knows her way around. Anyway, I did what was right, I sent her packing. I don't stand for any funny goings-on while I am in charge.'

As soon as she decently could Emily went back to her nurseries. She found Lettuce reading by the fire.

'Could you lend Polly a hand for a few days? I want to go home for a little holiday.'

That was no joyful home-coming.

'I wondered if you knew,' Betty said when she met Emily at the carrier's cart. 'We're expecting it in May.'

'But she's so young,' said Emily. 'He was taking advantage.'

'He's only young too, Sarah says. The silly girl says she thought they were marrying.'

'What's Dad say?'

'Nothing except he always did think Sarah was a bad girl. It won't make any difference to him, it's me will have all the work and just as things seemed easier. For as soon as the child's born Sarah will have to find herself a new place. I can't be doing with her here, for even when Albert and Henry wed there's no room.'

Sarah took care that Emily never caught her alone. She might be in disgrace but she had not lost her pride.

'Come the summer,' she told Betty, 'I shall go to London and find myself a place and it won't be in service. I am not spending my life bobbing to the gentry. I shall be gentry myself one day, you'll see.'

Emily had a feeling that Betty, though she never said so, rather admired Sarah's independence. It was to Emily silly talk but maybe it kept Sarah's spirits up.

That was a wonderful Christmas for Emily. The weather was nearly always kind so there was scarcely a day when she did not see Dick. On Christmas Eve they exchanged little gifts. Dick had a red felt strawberry filled with emery for Emily.

'It stops your needles rusting,' he told her. 'My Gran has one and when I saw it – summer it was – I thought that would be right for Emily is fond of needling.'

Emily had made a handkerchief for Dick with a 'D' embroidered on the corner. Dick knew he would never use it for it was much too beautiful.

One day there was a party at another house. It was for little children so Lady Reeve took Matthew and Lucy.

'If you could spare Polly,' Lady Reeve said to Emily, 'I can manage perfectly, and I expect you will be glad of an afternoon off.'

It was that afternoon when, for the only time, she and Dick had a real talk and, come to that, a real kiss. They sat in Dick's hut and he held her hands and told her his plans.

'I do see you can't leave Master Matthew yet but then I haven't spoke for a cottage yet, but I know I can have one. But some time Master Matthew will go to school same as the others and Miss Lucy is growing up, they won't need you then.'

Emily had thought this out.

'It all rests on Master Matthew, he should be going to

school two years come Michaelmas but it might be Doctor will say to hold him back.'

Dick laughed at her.

'What a one you are for ifs and an's. Supposing I spoke to Sir about the cottage?'

Emily was flustered.

'Oh, not yet!'

'Well, I'll let him get this Coronation over first and then I'll speak. I'll say I'm planning to wed, but not wed to who.'

Emily pressed against him.

'I do love you, Dick, truly I do. Tell me again about the chicks we'll have in our front garden.'

'I'd rather tell you about the babies you'll rear. Did you never think, Emily, that some day you would be holding your own baby in your arms?'

Emily thought about that.

'No. Funny thing is, I never did. I thought I was born to raise other people's little-uns.'

Thomas went off to school with John and Henry, apparently without a care in the world, except to be sure his tuck-box was as full of good things as his brothers'. Not, as Lettuce pointed out, that anyone would know what Thomas was feeling, no one ever did.

It felt empty in the house when the three boys had gone,

especially for Mary, for Matthew, owing to his delicacy, was not much of a companion for her. But there was plenty for Emily to do even though Lucy was now doing a full morning's lessons. The most important work Emily had on hand was making the girls' Coronation frocks. These were to be muslin over silk slips, as they had heard; Mary's was to be pink and Lucy's blue. The muslin frocks were to be very elaborate, covered in little tucks and lace insertions. It was close work and demanded her full attention, and had to be kept away from the girls who would finger it. But, of course, she thought as she worked, and much of her thinking was of Dick. Could it really come true, their own little cottage, their own garden full of flowers, their own chicks and, some day, their own baby? If she was lucky the mistress would allow her to take some of the baby clothes with her. It would be a wondrous thing if her baby could wear, as his first long robe, the one she had first dressed John in.

Just as the last stitch was put in the Coronation dresses a letter came from Betty. Sarah's baby had arrived. It was a girl and she had called it May after the month. The rest of the letter was about the Coronation, the most important news being that an ox was to be roasted whole. It seemed the ox was far more important in Easden than the King himself.

There were of course Coronation plans at Longton Place. A party for the tenants, which also included an ox roasted whole, but, as far as the village was concerned, the

edge was taken off the excitement because the family would
be away.

In those last weeks before they left for The Hall there was
growing excitement in the schoolroom.

'I don't like it,' Emily confided to Lettuce, 'getting
altogether above themselves they are, already I can feel the
tears.'

'It's only early June,' Lettuce comforted. 'You can't say
tears before bedtime yet.'

What was planned for The Hall was a village party with
an ox roasted whole on the Coronation day, then, on the day
after when the family returned, a supper in a huge marquee
on the lawn with fireworks afterwards.

The Burton family were to arrive first and for their arrival
the Baronet, who was as excited as a child, had decided to run
the flag to the top of the flag-pole. The flag-pole had been
erected on the top of the house and from it was to fly a vast
Union Jack. Such men as could be spared were in charge of
this arrangement under the supervision of Mr Binstead, the
head gardener. The drive was straight for a quarter of a mile
before it reached the house, so it was easy to time the arrival
of the wagonette.

'There they be,' said Mr Binstead as the two horses came
into view. 'Start to haul her up, boys.'

The boys tried to do as they were bidden but somehow the
rope had caught on the top of the pole.

'Drat her!' said Mr Binstead. Then he looked round for help. 'Dick lad, up the pole and let her free.'

By now the wagonette had almost stopped and the whole family were gazing up to see the flag fly. But what greeted them was a terrifying crack and the sight of Dick's body hurtling through the air to land with the neck broken by the front steps.

There was a pause there in Emily's story. Lucy said that all her life Emily saddened around the date Dick was killed. At that time nobody appears to have known that Dick's death meant anything to Nannie. She seems mercifully to have been stunned by what had happened. In any case there was so much to do. The luggage to come up, the unpacking to see to. If anyone spoke of Dick's death Emily did not remember it.

'Why should they?' she said to Lucy. 'It was sort of hushed up like. The Baronet didn't want anything said to upset the great occasion. There was so much going on even I had no time to think. New cousins and uncles and aunts to meet and the children getting wilder every minute. Then came the news. Of course it was sad the King having to have that operation but the upset was terrible. Miss Mary was not the only little girl who never forgave the King. It was the frock, you see, she had set her heart on it. It was no good our saying there would be plenty of occasions to wear the frock, parties and that, but she would not listen, she stamped and raged then lay on the floor sobbing. We did try saying that piece her grandmama had given her about a woman moved being like a fountain troubled, but she wouldn't listen and I don't wonder. I never understood it myself. But somehow the real burst of temper over the Coronation seemed to have got temper out of Miss Mary's system, it acted like a dose of gregory powder on an upset stomach. She was cross sometimes and a rare one for getting out of bed on the wrong side, but that was the last of the lying on the floor and screaming attacks, so I suppose it was a case of it's an ill wind that blows nobody any good.'

Back home Emily said life somehow settled down again as it always did if you tried your best and left things to God. With only three children in the house the time had come to reduce the nursery staff. It must have been difficult for Emily to decide what was right, dulled with grief as she was, for she would have felt as if she was struggling through a damp, dark wood, not able to see where her next step would take her. There was so much to consider, if only she could clear her wits. Was it right to leave Master Matthew? They said he would go to school when the time came, but would Doctor let him go? Miss Sylvia wouldn't think of that, she'd be thinking of the money saved if there was no head nurse to pay.

Then, just before Christmas, Polly, all of a dither, told her that she was to be married. It was to one of the footmen at The Hall, Peter, him that Mr Johnstone was training up to be under butler. Polly had not spoken of it before because there was no cottage, but now there was one and, please, she would like to leave right away.

'Oh, Nannie,' Polly said, happiness shining from her, 'he is such a lovely man.'

So Polly left and Annie stepped into her place and Mrs Smith let whoever could be spared help with the nursery trays. That Christmas Sylvia and Tom went away on a visit but the children stayed at home. Emily knew it would be bad news for the staff that the nursery would have to be looked after, so she suggested to Mrs Smith that the Christmas meals should be served in the dining-room to save tray carrying. Mrs Smith was shocked at the suggestion. What, all those dust sheets to come off and newspapers taken away from across the windows, it would be more trouble than it was worth!

Nannie, struggling to recall that Christmas, remembered the boys being home and the card games they played. She did say that John was a rare one for feeling things and that often, of an evening, he would come and sit on the floor at her feet, not saying anything but somehow being a comfort.

It was in February that Lettuce said:

'What we want is a bit of excitement. The house is so quiet with the boys away.'

It seemed as if Lettuce had scarcely spoken when excitement, if you could call it that, happened.

Right in the middle of term, without a word of warning, Thomas was brought home from school by Mr Tomkins himself.

All three boys had their own rooms and Thomas was ordered by Tom to go to his and stay there until he had permission to come out.

Nannie heard this from Annie who was always the first with news. She had been told that a plate of sandwiches and the drink tray had been taken by Mr Beck into the study.

There was never much food in the nursery, just milk, biscuits and cocoa and such things. Emily cared nothing for her master's ruling. Thomas was one of her nurslings and was not going to sit in a cold bedroom with no food in him. She made a jug of cocoa and filled a plate with biscuits and went to Thomas's room.

Still wearing his overcoat he was lying on his bed. It was hard to read his expression but whatever he had done he did not look repentant. Emily put the food by the bed.

'Drink the cocoa, dear, it will warm you.'

With a howl like an injured animal Thomas was clinging to her.

'Don't let Papa beat me, they don't know I did it, they only think I did. That policeman doesn't absolutely know.'

Policeman! A stab of fear ran through Emily. What could Master Thomas have done?

'Drink that cocoa,' she said gently unclasping Thomas's hands. 'Why, you're cold as ice. Now, not another word, just drink it up.'

All Nannie's children obeyed her. Thomas drunk the cocoa and she was glad to see some colour come into his cheeks.

'Could you stay, Nannie,' he pleaded, 'and come down with me when I'm sent for?'

Emily managed a smile.

'Somebody's forgetting they're eight. Too old to have a hand held. No, dear, I'm going back to my nursery. If you are sent to bed I'll be down later to see you.'

Emily never talked much about Thomas's crime. It seemed it was his usual trouble, wanting to draw attention to himself, but this time he had gone too far. He had set fire to another boy's bed, planning to stage a rescue scene in which he was the hero. Unfortunately for Thomas he had tried too hard and the papers and boxes he had arranged caught fire too quickly and reached the curtains and the fire brigade had to be summoned. It took the brigade no time to draw attention to what they called arson, for among the papers and boxes and other things used two belonged to Master Thomas Burton.

Nannie supposed a lot of talk went on about what to do

with Thomas. Mr Tomkins would not have him back. In the end it was decided he should finish the term working with Lettuce, but next term he would have a tutor to coach him for the entrance exam for his public school. All schools were alike to Emily, nasty places where little boys were locked away from their parents, so she did not grasp what it meant when she was told that Thomas would go to a different school from his brothers.

'As long as it's a nice school,' she said, 'it might be a good idea. Master Thomas was always so sharp. We don't want him doing better than John.'

Because he was to be kept at home Thomas was not to think that life would be easier than it was at school. He would not have his meals in the nursery with the girls and Matthew, he would have them in the schoolroom with Lettuce. He would have two hours exercise in the afternoons, and then two hours more lessons after tea. He would then go to his room for the night.

Lady Reeve, who had heard the bad news about Thomas in a letter from Tom, came at once to stay. She approved of the arrangements made but suggested she should help with finding a suitable tutor.

'He must be a true Christian able not only to educate Thomas but bring him up with Gawd as his guide.'

Only Emily seemed to think that Thomas's punishment was rather harsh. He was barely eight and though, of course, he had to be punished, to be permanently in disgrace seemed to her hard. However, it was not her place to criticise so she did not voice her opinion even to Lady Reeve.

Lady Reeve brought with her a suggestion from the Baronet. He thought it might help if, during the school terms, Thomas lived at The Hall. He could then himself see the boy was brought up a little sportsman. He had told his wife to tell Sylvia that he would be responsible for the tutor's salary.

Lettuce now came up to the nursery more rarely. The children being older there was more work for her to do. Mary had piano lessons in the afternoons, and after tea she had lessons to study and set for the next day. Both girls now learned needlework while Thomas and Matthew read or wrote an essay. Somehow every minute of the day seemed full.

When she did see Nannie Lettuce tried not to grumble, for there had been a look about Nannie ever since they had come back from The Hall last summer that made her wonder. For lack of better words she called it a shut-away look, but when she decided the time had come for her to leave she just had to talk things over.

'I've got to think of the future. In about six years Mary will be a young lady and be presented and all that. That will only leave Lucy and though, of course, she's still got a long way to go she too will grow up one day. Times are changing, people expect governesses to have some training, but there are still girls as untrained as I am in some of these schools for young ladies like the one I was at. I thought, if I could get a situation like that, I could go to night school and study to pass a teacher's examination.'

'I thought you had a certificate or something,' said Emily. 'With you able to play the piano and all.'

Lettuce laughed.

'My piano playing is of a very low standard. It's lucky neither Mary nor Lucy are musical or they would have passed me ages ago. And my needlework! You wait, I expect when I go the tutor will come here to teach all the children, then the mistress will ask you to take the girls for sewing. You'll see what my sewing is like.'

Lettuce left that summer, she had found a suitable situation teaching smaller children in a day school for gentlewomen near London.

She had also found somewhere to live. For years she kept up with Emily, telling her of her success when she passed the teacher's examination and of the good position she had got as a result.

The tutor did not come to Longton Place, instead they all moved to The Hall. Quite suddenly someone whose land marched with Tom's wanted to buy Longton Place and, after a lot of discussion with his lawyers, Tom sold.

'It's been hard going to keep it up,' he told Sylvia. 'People won't work like they did and expect more money for doing less. We'll go to The Hall to start with and look out for a smaller place without any farming land, then we'll stay around a bit and see how things turn out.'

The move made a lot of work for Emily. Packing her own and the children's possessions and, in the middle of it all, she had a letter from Betty who said, amongst family news, that Sarah had gone off with her Irish boy. She had left May with Betty. Sarah said she was going to marry her boy but Betty did not believe that, him coming from so grand a family.

'I must go home sometime,' Emily thought. 'I'd dearly love to cuddle that baby.'

The tutor chosen by Lady Reeve was all she had hoped for. A good, patient teacher, well up in Latin and Greek, which Thomas and Matthew would need for their entrance exams. Above all he was not only a Christian but thinking of being an ordinand. He was on even more intimate terms with Gawd than Lady Reeve herself.

The Baronet loathed the tutor. Psalm-singing milk sop, he called him, so, to counteract his effect, he undertook exercising Thomas himself. This would have worked well only it was decided Matthew should join in.

'Good for him,' said the Baronet, 'weedy little fellow. Soon put some muscle on him.'

Emily went off for her short holiday as soon as John and Henry went back to school. John was now at his public school. He wore more formal clothes but otherwise was unchanged. Still his quiet self, clinging to the quiet rhythm of nursery life. He talked sometimes to Emily about Longton Place which he had hated to leave.

'It was home, Nannie, which this house will never be. When I went away the things I had left in my bedroom were always there when I came back the next holiday, now I don't even know I'll sleep in the same room.'

Emily made a mental note to talk to Mrs Honeysett about that. To John she said:

'You wait and see. Like enough your room will be kept just as it is until you come back, it's not right crossing bridges until you come to them. You'll see, it will all be Sir Garnet.'

The Baronet had a new idea for exercising Thomas. They would play hare and hounds. He would be the hare for he could lay a trail in the morning at his own speed. Thomas and Matthew would be the hounds.

It was understood that Matthew would not run all the way if he did not feel like it and not at all if he felt wheezy. But Matthew hated being treated as an invalid so always he struggled on.

Emily knew nothing about the games played in the afternoons for it was then she took her walk. A sad little pilgrimage re-walking where she and Dick had walked. Later Emily was to tell Lucy: 'They say time is a great healer. I don't hold with that. Time covers over but it doesn't heal.'

It was lovely weather when Emily arrived at Easden. Betty, with May in the baby carriage, was waiting to greet her. None of the boys was home for they were all out working. She was, as usual, full of interest in Emily's doings.

'I was proper upset to hear Longton Place was to be sold, there's too much selling of the big houses. I don't know what the gentry do with their money. One moment there's stables of horses and a big staff and the next they're building something small – or what they call small – but always it means less staff. I don't know where it will end.'

'Sir Gerald and Lady Reeve still seem comfortable,' said Emily, 'no saving of pennies in that house.'

'But it's not the same as having your own place.'

Emily thought about that.

'I'm in the old nurseries, same as always. Well, they've always been the nurseries. Mrs Burton's Nannie, Nannie Ludgrove, her that died – I wrote you about that – well, she brought up all her children in those nurseries and I wouldn't wonder if Sir Gerald was brought up there too. Of course I don't use the night nursery now, not as a night nursery that is, it's smaller than our own at Longton Place so I've made it my room, it'll take time but I'll get it just as I want it in the end. Already I've got a nice screen I'm covering with pictures and that I've saved. It looks homely somehow.'

That night the dog-cart, with horses all of a lather, drew

up at the lodge gates. Betty heard the horses and came running out.

'I'm to fetch Nannie back to The Hall,' the driver told her. 'Little lad 'as took terrible bad and is asking for her.'

Playing hare and hounds the two boys had been caught in a cloud-burst. There was no shelter so they pushed on. Back at The Hall Lady Reeve at once ordered hot baths and hot drinks but the wet had soaked into Matthew. The next day he was down with pneumonia.

Emily would not let Lady Reeve get a nurse. 'I can manage with Annie. He'll try harder for me than he would for a stranger.' And what a fight Emily and Matthew put up. During the crisis, when Matthew's temperature had risen so high he was barely conscious, when he was blue in the face and shaken by a hacking cough, the doctor, who had stayed the night, had to warn Emily he couldn't live.

'Poor little fellow! He can't live, Nannie. Maybe it's cruel to go on trying.'

'He will live,' Emily said quietly. 'Can I give him another sponge down?'

The doctor nodded.

'When he picks at the bed-clothes, that's usually the end.'

'Then he won't pick at them,' said Emily.

Two days later Matthew's temperature suddenly dropped. And two hours later, in a whisper, he said he was hungry. Emily had always been famous for a broth she made. It had a steak basis, she called it 'Golden Sovereigns'. Now she had a bowl of it waiting and spooned some into Matthew's mouth.

The doctor, who arrived at that minute, would have startled his patients if they had seen him dance a few steps of the Cake Walk chanting: 'We've done it, Nannie. We've done it or rather you have, God bless you.'

Naturally that was not the end. Stimulants still had to be at hand for Matthew was so weak he could easily slip away.

Tom and Sylvia were away while Matthew was so ill, but of course they were informed. On their return to The Hall Lady Reeve said:

'When you go up to see Matthew don't forget to thank Nannie. The doctor says but for her Matthew would have died.'

Sylvia gave an amused laugh.

'How doctors do exaggerate!'

Matthew's illness was the last nursery drama. Much to his joy he was not sent to Mr Tomkins but was kept at home studying with the tutor for the next six years, so did not go away to school until he was thirteen. By that time Thomas was at his public school, so Lady Reeve most regretfully decided her good Christian tutor would have to go, and the girls should have a French governess, not so much for lessons as for polish. So a pretty Mademoiselle Moulin was installed who taught them to talk French, to dance, to make a Court curtsey and what the Baronet called 'other fripperies'.

Tom and the Baronet were deeply involved at that time by the Territorial Force, the Baronet as honorary colonel and Tom as commanding officer. Sylvia thought it was a nuisance, grown men playing at soldiers.

The boys were grown up. John went to Cambridge and Henry to Oxford where he had been awarded a scholarship. Thomas was an anxiety but his school literally beat him into some sort of shape. Each holiday he would rush up to Emily to show her the marks on his backside of the latest beatings, but for Thomas, though she was sorry for him, there was no sympathy. 'If you'd behaved right you wouldn't have suffered.'

Lady Reeve was getting very crippled with rheumatics but she often managed to find her way to Nannie's room for a nice talk. In the evenings Nannie would send Annie downstairs to have fun in the servant's hall and she would be sitting in her armchair, her work-basket beside her, mending.

'Funny,' she would say, 'now I'm only sewing for Miss Mary and Miss Lucy there seems just as much work as before when I had a nursery full.'

It was at one of these evening talks that Nannie learnt that she was to lose Annie.

'This summer Miss Mary is to be presented. She is to stay

with her aunt in London for the season. She will, of course, need a maid so I thought Annie could look after her.'

Emily could not visualise a presentation so she spoke about what she knew.

'That will be easy, M'Lady. After all, Miss Lucy is fourteen and needs no looking after except maybe a hand with buttons at the back, and that Mademoiselle can do. I shall see to the mending as I always have and perhaps Mrs Honeysett will provide a girl to turn out my nursery and bring up the trays and that.'

Lady Reeve agreed with a nod.

'But that brings us to what I wanted to say. I don't want any changes. I want you to keep your own room but we have to look forward. In a year or two the older children will be getting married and one day, please Gawd, will be coming to stay with babies of their own. They will need you then.'

'They will have Nannies of their own, M'Lady.'

'They will need you but perhaps we will have to change your name. When that happens I shall call you Gran-Nannie.'

PART FIVE

Gran-Nannie

John was the first to bring a bride to visit Emily. He knocked on her door and called out:

'Nannie, it's John, can I bring someone to visit you?'

He led in a shy girl called Alice. It was a cold morning so Emily made her sit by the fire.

'You must have some of my Golden Sovereigns, I made it directly I heard you were coming. It's keeping hot in this saucepan.'

She poured out two cups full of her famous soup. Under its warming influence Alice relaxed slightly. She showed Nannie her engagement ring.

'I know how well you've brought him up,' she said. 'I'm afraid you may find me very inexperienced.'

Emily studied the girl.

'Can you needle?'

'We had a German governess who made us all make samplers using all the different stitches, later my stepmother tried to teach us to embroider and I think she found me very clumsy.'

'Alice's mother died when she was four,' John explained.

Emily looked at the girl with kindness.

'If you want any help with your needling you come to me.'

Then John told Emily his personal news.

'I have decided what I want to do, Nannie. I am going to be ordained.'

'So some day,' Alice said, 'I am going to be a rector's wife. I do hope I'm more sensible by then. For I want to be good at it, you know, visiting people when they are ill and all that.'

'Her Ladyship is pleased, isn't she?'

John flushed.

'You're the only one who knows. We came straight up here. I will tell her this evening.'

John's was not the first family wedding. Mary's was. She became engaged in her first season to a brilliant young lawyer who, prophets said, would become a judge. Mary was head over heels in love but was strangely unwilling to fix the date of the wedding. Nobody understood this but Nannie. Lady Reeve wanted a summer wedding and was longing to start preparations, but Mary would not decide on a date but would shut herself up in the room she shared with Lucy, gossiping and laughing. Then one evening Mary came up to the nursery. After a good deal of beating about the bush she said:

'Do you think I could take Lucy with me when I get married?'

Nannie showed no surprise because she felt none.

'No, dear,' she said in a firm voice, 'it wouldn't do. When a young lady marries she doesn't take her sister with her.'

'But I shan't know anybody where we are going to live and Louis will be away all day, if Lucy was there I could have fun.'

'You'll have plenty to do,' Emily comforted. 'The meals to order and flowers to arrange and you could take up something like young ladies do. Miss Alice is learning what they call Home Nursing, always come in handy, that will.'

'If after I've been married a little while I have a baby will you come and look after it?'

Emily shook her head.

'You can't have me either, getting married is something you do by yourself. When the time comes you'll have a Nannie of your own and you'll be teaching your own little 'uns all that about "a woman moved". You'll do all right, dear. Now give Nannie a kiss and run along. It's time for Bedfordshire.'

Mary had a lovely wedding when all the azaleas were in flower. She looked a picture swathed in lace and so did the bridesmaids who were dressed in pink.

That was the first time Emily appeared in a black silk apron, a garment she wore for the rest of her life. There were several child bridesmaids and pages and, though they all had their own attendants, Lady Reeve put Nannie in charge. So, under a tree some way from the wedding party, all the child attendants were given nursery tea and strawberries and cream.

'No, dear, we don't start with strawberries, we have two pieces of bread and butter. No, dear, we don't get up in the middle of tea. If your mama wants you she'll know where to find you. That's not a nice way to talk, dear, don't care was made to care, don't care lost a duck. Now, no squabbling, little birds in their nests agree.'

Lady Reeve sailed down on the tea-party.

'Splendid!' she said. 'Don't forget grace, children, we must thank Gawd for this lovely day.' Then, looking at the pink-clad little girls, she said to Emily: 'These bridesmaids' frocks so put me in mind of the one Miss Mary had hoped to wear for the Coronation.'

Emily's heart turned over but she said firmly:

'Yes indeed, M'Lady.'

John's wedding was a much quieter affair. The King had died recently and the country was still in mourning, and a quiet wedding was what both John and Alice wanted.

The night before John came up to the nursery to say goodbye to Emily. He found her ironing some small things for Alice. He was soon to be ordained and would go as curate to an uncle in Kent.

'We are going to be very poor, Nannie. Papa has some money but it's tied up. He'll give me an allowance as he always has done, but it won't be much; if we need advice can Alice ask you?'

'You won't need advice, dear, it will all be Sir Garnet.'

John took the iron away from Nannie and gently pushed her into her armchair.

'I don't think you will understand this, but I pray to God that when we have children they are brought up as you brought us up.'

Emily hesitated.

'You'll have a Nannie no doubt but she won't need to look after your babies the way I looked after you. You see, Miss Alice will be a motherly mother, that's something you can't teach anybody. Your mama is a different sort. She loves you in her own way but not my way.'

John knelt down by the armchair and put his arms round Emily.

'Bless you, dearest Nannie. Every day I thank God for you in my prayers.'

No newspaper ever came into Emily's nurseries and she seldom talked with the rest of the staff, so the news that the country was at war came as a surprise to her. As she went about her tasks she pondered about this war. Would it be like that Boer War that the master had gone to? Now she came to think of it she supposed that it was because of this war that the master and the Baronet were always dressing up and going out drilling. Not, of course, that the Baronet could fight in a war, he was too old, but what about the master? It was to be hoped he did not go for a soldier again – look how it had upset the mistress last time. Of course Miss Mary's husband would not go, what would a legal gentleman do in an army?

The war came nearer home for Emily when Henry came to see her. He was now a City gentleman and, so Lady Reeve said, 'making a lot of money'. Whenever he came to stay at The Hall his first call was always on Emily. Usually he rushed in and rushed out, but this time he sat on the arm of her chair.

'I'm going to get married, Nannie,' he paused, then he said in a proud voice, 'to Miss Billie Day.'

The name meant nothing to Emily.

'That's nice, dear, but what a funny name for a young lady.'

'She's an actress, Nannie, a very famous one.'

'Never mind, dear, she can give that up now she's marrying you. Can she needle?'

'I don't know,' Henry confessed, 'but Grandmama is not going to approve and I do want her to like her. You see I've joined the Army and I would like her to come here sometimes when I am away.'

'Why haven't you brought the young lady here so Her Ladyship can meet her?'

Henry thought about Billie, with her late nights and staying in bed half the morning.

'I told you, she's an actress, they aren't free in the day time, having photographs taken and things, but I could bring her on Sunday. I have bought a motor-car, Nannie.'

Emily had not even seen a motor-car but she had heard about them. She had stuck a picture on her screen of a lady in a big motoring hat tied under her chin with a silk veil, wearing a long coat called a dust coat. She looked fondly at Henry. He was such a clever boy, why could he not see he could not bring this actress lady to call on a Sunday in a motor-car?

'If I were you, dear, I would talk to your grandpapa. He will know the best way for your young lady to meet Her Ladyship.'

The Baronet was proud of Henry. Funny sort of job he had but the late King had introduced businessmen into society. You did not necessarily like them but you accepted them. Anyway he was delighted that Henry had joined the Forces. As for this little actress, she would probably pass, but he could not say that to Henry so he suggested a compromise. As he had this motor-car why not bring the girl down on Saturday night? If Henry could persuade her to be up in time for matins good, if not Her Ladyship, bless her, must put up with it.

Emily sat up to welcome Henry and Billie. She had a saucepan full of Golden Sovereigns waiting. Johnstone, the butler, was getting old so the first footman, Peter who had married Polly, let them in. Nobody knows what Emily expected an actress to look like but, with the sympathy which was natural to her, she greeted her as she would any girl who was going to marry one of her boys, and this was certainly a pretty one.

'How do you do, dear, come and sit by the fire and drink some of my Golden Sovereigns, you must be cold and tired.'

Then, after Billie had sipped a little of the soup, she asked: 'Can you needle?'

Henry had told Billie a lot about his Nannie. Billie came from a theatrical family and had practically been born in a theatre basket but she had fine parents. Money was often tight but they managed to send her to a good school.

'Oh yes,' she said in answer to Nannie's question. 'Sewing was my best thing at school. You see, I went to a convent.'

Emily felt quite funny. An actress Her Ladyship just might accept but a convent she never would.

Henry sensed what Emily was thinking.

'I've told Billie about Grandmama and convents and we are keeping it a secret.'

Emily nodded in approval.

'Very sensible, Miss Billie, what the eye does not see the heart does not grieve after. Now finish your soup, Master

Henry, and then I'll show Miss Billie her room for it's time for Bedfordshire.'

Henry and Billie were married by special licence before he was sent to France. He was home on leave just once before he was killed. He could not, he said, stay at The Hall for Billie's musical play was doing enormous business, but he came down for a day.

As usual his first call was on Nannie. He had changed, she noticed, looking somehow as if there was wire instead of bones inside him. He did not, she thought, look fit to go back to those trenches.

'Could you see Doctor, dear? I think he'll tell you that you need a rest.'

He clung to her then as if he was a baby again. He gave a dreary sort of laugh.

'Oh, Nannie, you'll never know what it's like and I thank God you don't. It's hell, just plain hell. Nobody can have rest until it's over.' Then, still holding her, he whispered: 'I'm not coming back again, Nannie, it's a miracle I've survived so far. Billie thinks we might be having a baby, if we do, will you help her, Nannie?'

Nannie let her soothing syrup of phrases pass through her mind and dismissed them all. This was not a time for 'It will be all Sir Garnet.'

'Don't fret, dear. You tell Miss Billie, if I'm wanted, she has only to let me know.'

It was soon after Henry's death that John's two children came to stay at The Hall, girls called Isobel and Victoria. Even with the small allowance that Tom was able to give them John and Alice were very poor. It was not considered possible that people in their position had no staff, so there was a young Nannie, a cook-general and a house parlourmaid. Isobel and Victoria were sent to The Hall because Alice was having another baby. The children were too small to travel alone so Lady Reeve suggested Sylvia should collect them.

Sylvia had seen that as her children married there would be grandchildren who needed looking after, so she had made preparations. She had stayed for a long time with one of her sisters who was an enthusiastic V.A.D. and had become trained herself. She rather fancied herself with a red cross on her apron and a white cap flying from her head, but she had no stomach for nursing. Instead she had found herself the perfect task. Longton Place was handed over by its new owners to be a hospital and with it went Sylvia as commandant. So, when an escort was needed for the two little girls, Sylvia was sorry she could not help but the hospital must come first. 'We never know when a convoy is coming.'

To Emily the drive to the Kent village where John and Alice lived was a great excitement for it would give her a chance to see John. The house they lived in was a shock because it was not a gentleman's residence, just a little house in the village street, and just a small garden, no stable or anything, not that Master John needed stables for he was not carriage folk. Emily was no snob but it did not seem right somehow.

But John had not changed, he came running out, his clergy collar giving him a different look somehow. His face was shining with happiness.

'Nannie, dearest Nannie.'

Alice, though she was enormous and could not get about much, had cooked a nice lunch and over it Emily heard the news.

'John can never get away, not even for a night.'

'Well, you see, Nannie, I never know who is going to get a telegram next and I must be ready to comfort if I can.'

The little girls, though they had never been away from home before, left quite happily with Emily. Their father, as he lifted them into the dog-cart, said:

'Now, this is my Nannie, so she is your Gran-Nannie.'

Shyly the children replied:

'How do, Gran-Nannie.'

Perhaps because they were John's babies Nannie especially loved Isobel and Victoria. She had a bed for herself put into the old day nursery, and the children's cots placed on either side, and all meals were served at the old nursery table.

'It was about the last time the nursery was properly waited on,' Nannie would remember, 'for the young maids went away to make munitions and such and they never came back.' On that visit the children did not talk much though through them Emily saw signs of her training. Nice table manners and no upraised voices, and one day Isobel said, putting a tiny portion of her pudding to one side: 'Leave something for Mr Manners.'

Nannie might not approve of what she had to say but she knew her duty.

'We don't give Mr Manners anything any more, dear, not in war-time, for ships like the one Uncle Thomas is in have to fetch our food for us and sometimes they get sunk.'

The next children to come to stay were Mary's eldest, a boy and a girl. Mary had been an orderly little girl except for her temper and now she was an orderly mother; she was to have six children properly arranged: boy, girl, boy, girl, all down the line. She and Louis were much better off than John and Alice. She must have been miserable with Louis fighting in France and terrified, as were most women, of a telegram, but she would not accept Lady Reeve's offer of a home at The Hall while the war lasted. She felt she must have her own home ready for Louis if he came on leave.

Emily, remembering those days, had to admit that Miss Mary's children were better dressed than Master John's and were beautifully brought up.

'And no wonder,' she said. 'I met their Nannie for she brought the children to us, she put me in mind of Nannie Ludgrove. I can't say higher than that.'

Against all expectations Matthew got into the Forces. He had been determined that he would and put off applying until he saw his chance. He could never pass a medical for the infantry, but he was accepted as a medical orderly. Lady Reeve was annoyed.

'Stupid boy, he's much too delicate to be of any use.'

But Emily understood.

'He was never one to want favours on account of him not being strong.'

Emily, shut away in the old nurseries with mending piled up round her, would think a lot. No good worrying about the war, those who were taken were taken, it was the living she thought about. Already her brothers, Albert, Tom and Fred were gone. She could still see them crowded round the table at Easden, strange the way things turned out, reared in poverty, farm labourers while they were still children, only to be killed in France, a country they'd hardly heard tell of. But Sarah, who grew up much the same, was married to a Lord. Her husband was in the war too but if he came through he had a castle to go to, whereas if Albert, Tom or Fred had been spared it would have been back to farm labouring if they were lucky.

Emily's chief worry at that time was Miss Lucy. She was

a gentle girl always trying to be of use and there were plenty asking for her. Not a week went by but Miss Mary wrote. She was so lonely for now there were three babies in the nursery she scarcely saw her Nannie. She only saw the children when they came down after tea. Couldn't Lucy come and stay, they could have such fun together?

Then Lady Reeve had her claims. She had now become an old lady and no longer walked but was pushed about in a huge bath-chair. The Baronet, though older than she was, kept his straight back and his health. There were only two old gardeners: Binstead, who was really retired but had come back to help out, and a friend of his. They gave all their attention to the kitchen garden, so the Baronet would go around with a knife and some tools attempting to prune his roses or get a few weeds out of his drive. There was no question but that Lady Reeve could do with the services of a young able-bodied grand-daughter, for at that date when the gentry became old they allowed themselves to give up. Lady Reeve had her maid but she was as old as she was though, not being gentry, was expected to work. It was the ordinary things Lucy was needed for: letters to write, food to arrange, plans to be made, wages to be paid.

'Oh dear, Lucy, what would I do without you?' Lady Reeve would say. 'I thank Gawd every day for you.'

There was also Sylvia pleading for her daughter to be by

her side. Lucy could have no idea how lonely she was without your dear Papa. No one would ever know how she suffered when poor Henry was killed. The work of a commandant was terrible. If only Lucy were there to take some of the burden off her, and it really was Lucy's business to come to her, an unmarried daughter's place was with her mother.

Lucy took her problem to Emily.

'Well, dear, it's for you to say,' said Emily. 'Which would you like to do?'

Lucy was sure about that.

'Oh, I'd stay here. I feel I belong. But I suppose if Mama needs me . . .'

'It's not a question of needing,' said Emily, 'but I expect she's had enough. I'm surprised she has worked at it that long.'

'I wonder,' Lucy said hopefully, 'if Mama stops being a commandant if she would like to stay with Mary.'

Emily knew the answer to that.

'Miss Mary wouldn't want her.'

'Or she could come here.'

'It wouldn't do, dear,' Emily said. 'There's not enough going on.'

'What would you advise, Nannie? Please tell me.'

Emily looked lovingly at her youngest nursling.

'I'd think of myself for once. It isn't often you do that.'

'Then I'll stay here,' said Lucy. 'I'll write to Mama this very afternoon to tell her so.'

It sometimes seemed to Emily that nobody came home from the war or, if they did, they were so badly wounded they had to spend months in hospital being patched up before being sent out to France again. Polly's husband was one of these and so was the boy Annie had married, only hers could not be sent back because he had been blinded. Somehow Matthew survived for occasionally Emily got an official card from him which said he was well. Thomas was believed to be a prisoner-of-war, his ship had been sunk but the German ship had picked up survivors.

Food grew very scarce throughout the country. The full severity of this was not felt at The Hall for there were rabbits and sometimes a game-bird, but they heard all about it from Sylvia, who could always twist a situation to fit her own ends.

'The men here get plenty to eat but the women practically starve. The men say officers get the best of everything in France. Trust Tom.'

It was John's family who brought the food situation home. Poor Isobel was sent to The Hall to live for a while because, like Matthew, she had asthma. Emily took her to live in the old nurseries and there, besides struggling with the latest asthma crisis, she tried to feed the child up. To aid her to do this she stole a cow. The milk from all the cows was sent to a centre; enough was kept back for the needs of the house, which was a very small portion indeed. Lady Reeve might be an invalid but she still ruled her household.

'I will not have milk wasted on us,' she said, 'our wounded need it.'

So only enough for cups of tea reached the kitchen. It was known that a cow in milk was missing but nothing was said officially, for all knew that in an untended part of the garden the cow was tethered to be milked by Emily. Not one drop was wasted. Emily made butter and cheese and the kitchen made milk puddings. There was some flesh on little Isobel's bones and the whole household felt the better for Nannie's cow.

Then Victoria was sent to Emily. A poor diet had brought her out in boils.

In after years Victoria, who had a retentive memory, could describe what she and the other children called 'Gran-Nannie's' room. It was crowded with nicknacks the children had given her. Bought sometimes for Christmas and birthdays but often handmade. On the walls were texts with flowers painted round them. 'God is love,' with dog roses and 'Suffer the Little Children to come unto Me' with daisies. In pride of place there was a collection of small photographs mounted in a cardboard backing of six nurslings. Lady Reeve had given it to Emily. Woven around the photographs were the words: 'Make them to be numbered with Thy saints in glory everlasting.' Under the photograph of Henry was written 'numbered' and the date.

'How do you know Uncle Henry's a saint?' Victoria had asked Nannie. 'I mean, if I was killed in a war I wouldn't suddenly be a saint. I'd be just the same as I was a minute before.'

'He gave his life for his country,' Emily said, 'that makes him a saint.'

The third of John's family was sent to Emily. John brought her himself.

'She won't eat,' he explained. 'We've tried everything. Alice is exhausted. We even try hiding food under cushions and in chairs in the hope she'll find it and eat it.'

The child was skin and bone, not looking at all as a child should look.

'You leave her to me, Master John. All children eat in my nursery.'

So Louise ate.

Emily always said it was difficult to know when the war ended. Food went on being scarce and, instead of dying of wounds, people died of influenza. The Baronet was one of the first to die of it. He had gone out with his gun hoping to

get something for the pot. He succeeded in bringing home
a rabbit and a duck but, when he got into the house, he did
not take the birds to Johnstone but slumped into his chair
and dropped the game on the floor. Puzzled at not being
called Johnstone came to see what was happening.

'I don't know what's wrong,' the Baronet said, 'but I feel
queer, damn queer.'

Somehow old Johnstone, who was older than the Baronet,
got him to bed and Emily was fetched and the doctor
summoned, not as once by horse but by telephone, which
their children had insisted their parents had installed.

The doctor, having examined the Baronet, beckoned
Emily into the hall.

'It's this influenza. It's a killer. He's got a spot on his lung,
no bigger than a pin's head which, almost while I watch, will
become the size of a half-crown. We treat it as pneumonia
but it's nearly always a losing battle.'

It was certainly a losing battle for the Baronet who died
before the day was out, looking somehow faintly surprised
to find himself going.

All the children came for the funeral, amongst them
Sylvia and Tom. John took the service. Lady Reeve was
present, helped into her seat she sat upright and composed.
Afterwards she told her children it was Gawd's will.

Amongst those who attended the funeral was Billie. She
was, she told Emily, not working so she thought she should

drive down and pay her respects. Henry would have liked that. She had brought with her little Henry so that he might meet his grandparents. Grandparents! With a start Emily realised she was talking of Miss Sylvia and Mr Tom.

After the funeral Emily entertained little Henry while Billie got to know her relations. He was, Emily thought, a dear little boy, very like his father had looked at his age, but there were things about him which needed putting right, little habits that she would not allow in her nursery.

'Looks as though he could do with some of my Golden Sovereigns,' Emily said to Billie when she returned little Henry to her. 'We can't get the meat yet of course but when it's back maybe he could come for a visit. Her Ladyship would enjoy that.'

Matthew came to The Hall. He was at a loose end not having decided what he wanted to do. He looked terribly frail. Mysteriously he had caught the influenza and, as sometimes happened, he already so delicate, had survived, whereas the strong died in a matter of hours. He had become used to companionship during the war and wandered around the estate unable to settle to anything. Then one day he bounded up to the nursery as he had done when he was a little boy.

'Nannie! Nannie! I know what I'm going to do. Stay here, there's so much wants doing and since grandfather died there's no one to plan.'

'If you think you can do it, dear,' Emily said quietly, 'I think it would please your grandmama.'

Lady Reeve never grasped that she was trying to live in the past. She still talked as if there was a house full of servants. When any of the family were coming to stay, she would say:

'Will you tell Mrs Honeysett, Lucy dear, or should I see her?'

Lucy would reply:

'Oh I'll do it, darling. No need for you to bother.'

Never by an inflection did she suggest the truth, that Mrs Honeysett had died in the influenza epidemic.

In some ways Lady Reeve was lucky, the staff that she had was elderly. She would have found the young girls that some of her friends employed shockingly independent, completely unaware that they had a place and ought to stick to it.

To Gran-Nannie these were beautiful years, there always seemed to be children staying in the house and like their fathers and mothers before them they dashed up the stairs to fling themselves into Gran-Nannie's arms. She was becoming old and was not as nimble as she had been but when the next generation of children arrived she was still able to hold them on her knee and, jigging them up and down, croon 'A gee-gee and a gentleman, went out to ride one day.'

Nobody knew Gran-Nannie was ill. It was as if a flower withered and died. She never made a fuss so it was in keeping she should die quietly in her sleep.

She left a little note to Lucy expressing her wishes. She had saved all her life so now there was a nice little sum in a box under her bed.

'I want that for you children or your children if you should ever need it.'

On my gravestone I should like put: 'She hath done what she could.'

John took the funeral but he would not have his Nannie carried to the church in a hearse. Her arms had cradled them all as babies so she should be cradled by her babies now. It seemed a very small coffin but it was carried with love by John, young Henry, Thomas and Matthew, and Thomas and Matthew's two sons.

Such a simple life but no one who came under her influence ever forgot her.

'How we shall miss her,' Mary said to Lucy.

Lucy choked back a sob.

'Do you know what she would say to that?'

They smiled as if they would hear Nannie's voice and said together.

'It will all be Sir Garnet.'